LOOKING BACK: 1990

Nathaniel Harris

B. T. Batsford Ltd, London

LOOKING BACK
1990

Contents

© Nathaniel Harris 1991
First published 1991

All rights reserved. No part of this publication
may be reproduced, in any form or by any means,
without permission from the Publisher

Typeset by Tek-Art Ltd West Wickham Kent
and printed in Great Britain by
The Bath Press, Bath

Published by B.T. Batsford Ltd
4 Fitzhardinge Street, London W1H 0AH

A CIP catelogue record for this book is
available from the British Library

ISBN 7134 6767 3

Introduction

Great events seldom take place neatly within the limits of a calendar year; and 1990 was no exception. It ended, as it had begun, with all sorts of loose ends waiting to be tied up. The outstanding example was the 'Gulf crisis' which arose after Iraq's occupation of Kuwait in August 1990: five months later, on 31 December, it was still unclear whether the dispute between Iraq and the United Nations would be resolved peacefully, although the 15 January deadline was uncomfortably close. However, even the earliest readers of this introduction will know that war did break out, and also, almost certainly, how and when it ended.

Much that happened in 1990 can be traced back to three related developments that changed the world in the late 1980s: the far-reaching programme of reform and democratization initiated in the Soviet Union by Mikhail Gorbachev; the end of the Cold War and the growth of co-operation between the United States and the USSR; and the collapse of Communism in Eastern Europe. The chronology on page 58 demonstrates just how much of this process was crammed into the single year 1989.

The consequences were felt in all sorts of ways. But for the end of the Cold War, there would have been no united front, operating in the name of the United Nations, against Iraq. Whether this marked the beginning of a 'new world order', or a period of American world domination, remained in question. Severe economic problems had largely triggered the changes in the Soviet Union, and those same problems led it to abandon its impressive but expensive role as superpower protector of client states all over the world, from Cuba to Vietnam. This abdication made possible the overthrow of Communism in Eastern Europe and the momentous unification of Germany – in effect, the death of the Communist East German state.

May: Nelson and Winnie Mandela visit London for a concert in Wembley stadium.

Introduction

These and other events of 1990 underlined the utter failure of Communism. As free elections took place in one country after another, most voters rejected the one-party 'workers' states' that had ruled in their name for forty-odd years. A series of investigations revealed them to have been not only repressive, but inefficient and corrupt. And, perhaps most significant of all, even Communists openly or tacitly agreed: the outgoing president of Poland, General Jaruselski, formally apologized for the sufferings inflicted by Communism, and in several states the Communist Party more or less vanished, changing its name and radically revising its programme.

It now seemed clear beyond dispute that one-party systems, however well-intentioned, were less efficient and more corruptible than multi-party systems; these, whatever their faults, ensured that governments were ultimately accountable to those whom they governed, and gave different groups and conflicting interests some kind of political representation. The impact of these findings was felt far beyond the Communist bloc. In 1990 the largest Communist Party in non-Communist Europe – Italy's – changed its name and nature; and over huge areas of Africa, one-party systems were abandoned in the face of popular pressure.

Moreover, the part played in Eastern Europe by the mass demonstrations of 1989 seems to have boosted confidence in the ability of ordinary people to bring about political changes. In 1990 there was a continuing sense that they were on the move, whether in Africa, Albania, Nepal or Bangladesh, although China, in the aftermath of the Tiananmen Square massacre, was a notable exception. A sense that everything was going in one direction may also have contributed to the breakthrough in South Africa, where the government representing the white minority seemed at last ready to contemplate the possibility of an equal, multiracial society.

June: earthquake in Iran.

Introduction

October: the aftermath of the Temple Mount riots in Jerusalem.

Not all of the changes were entirely positive. National and ethnic conflicts, suppressed under Communism, flared up in many parts of Eastern Europe and the USSR. In these regions, centuries of migrations had mixed peoples up with one another; and now Armenians and Georgians, Uzbeks and Kazakhs, came to blows over claims to territory, while gypsies in Czechoslovakia, Albanians in Serbia, Hungarians in Romania and many other minorities had cause to complain of their treatment. And where large groups were concerned, nationalism threatened to break up entire states, with unforseeable consequences; at moments this seemed imminent in Czechoslovakia, where the Slovaks were in militant mood, and it was an ever-present possibility in the cases of the USSR and Yugoslavia.

Such problems complicated the already difficult situations in these countries, while creating democratic structures and dismantling state-run economies was already proving difficult enough in the face of economic problems and oil shortages caused by the Gulf crisis. Ironically, the USSR's first democratic leader, Mikhail Gorbachev, spent much of 1990 accumulating near-dictatorial powers with which to push through reforms and hold the state together. But here and in Eastern Europe, the basics of democratic politics seemed to have become established, as opposition, criticism and messy compromises replaced the enforced unity of the Communist state and the temporary unity of the anti-Communist alliance that overthrew it. In this sense, the divisions within Solidarity and the fraught, abusive nature of the Polish presidential elections were probably healthy signs.

Introduction

At a time when the USSR seemed to be falling apart, therw was a strong tendency elsewhere for countries to draw together in regional groupings. This was particularly apparent in Western Europe, where economic and even political union began to seem realistic possibilities for the European Community (EC). Her incautiously expressed hostility to these prospects helped to bring down one of the most forceful leaders of the 1980s, Britain's Margaret Thatcher.

In the Cold War, economic superiority had been a key factor in the triumph of the 'West' – a term that continued to be used to describe the advanced capitalist economies, although these actually included Japan and other non Euro-American states. In 1990 some Western countries were in fact experiencing difficulties which in Britain gave rise to gloomy predictions about future economic growth and employment levels. However, such problems appeared to be slight when compared with those of Eastern Europe and the Soviet Union, and non-existent by comparison with the poverty of the least developed (Third World) countries. These received some limited help in the form of reorganizations of their crippling debts, which were in many instances so large that they found it hard to pay the interest on them, and had no serious prospect of ever paying off the principal.

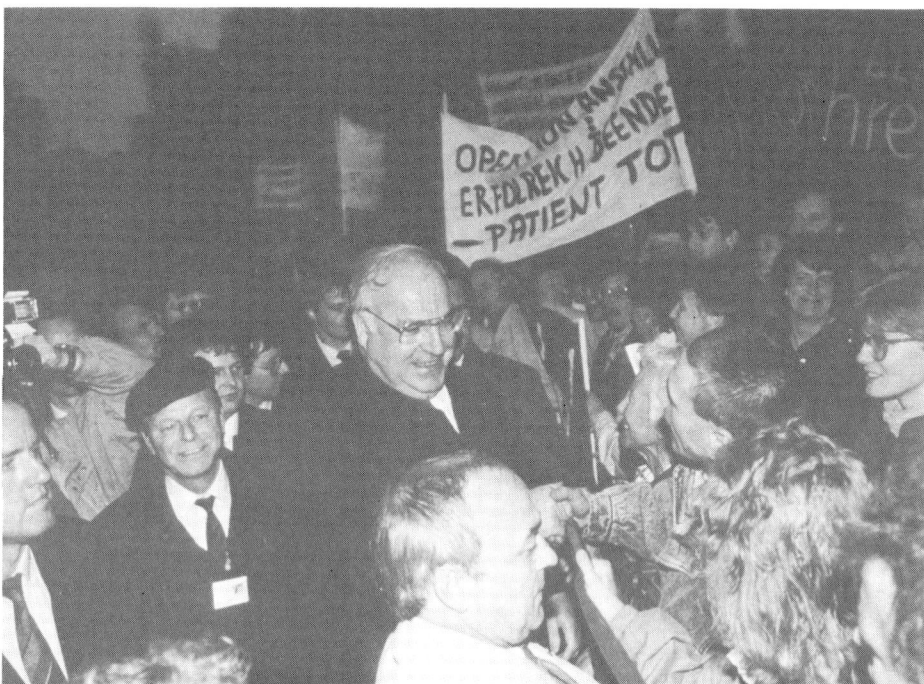

German Chancellor Helmut Kohl on the campaign trail.

Other long-term problems which received attention included the environment and AIDS. The many conferences and congresses held in 1990 were striking evidence of world concern at the destruction of the environment by human action; but opinions varied about the seriousness of the situation and the proper solutions. Nor was a cure found for AIDS, the condition which destroyed its victims' immune systems, condemning them to an almost certain early death. Already of epidemic proportions in Africa, AIDS affected ever-increasing numbers elsewhere. Governments financed campaigns to promote 'safe sex' (chiefly through the use of condoms), since AIDS was mainly acquired through sexual contact.

Introduction

John Major moves into 10 Downing Street.

Troop movements in the desert in December.

With the end of the Cold War, the former Communist bloc posed a new potential 'threat' – the threat of destabilizing the world through disasters such as economic collapse and mass emigration. Intractable, longer-lived issues included Hindu-Muslim antagonism in the Indian sub-continent, a seemingly unbreakable chain of killings in Northern Ireland, and the future of Palestine, unresolved despite the continuing unrest in Israel's Occupied Territories. Most sensationally of all, the Gulf crisis brought up a whole range of questions about the prospects for a peaceful international order, stability in the Middle East, the control of the arms trade and the industrialized world's dependence on oil. From this it seems evident that 1991, too, will have its full share of dramas and dilemmas.

BALTIC CRISIS

INITIATED by President Mikhail Gorbachev, the liberalization within the USSR and the relaxation of the Soviet grip on Eastern Europe continued to produce dramatic results.

Some of these appeared to threaten the very foundations of the USSR. As a federation, the Soviet Union consisted of a number of linked republics; but in the past, real power had always been wielded by the central government in Moscow. The new freedoms allowed separatist sentiments to be expressed, and these were particularly strong in Lithuania, Latvia and Estonia – three Baltic republics that had been independent until their bitterly resented annexation in 1940 by the USSR.

Lithuania took the lead in December 1989, when the Lithuanian Communist Party severed its links with the Soviet party. A declaration of national independence was clearly imminent, and the Soviet government reacted by sending a battery of high officials for discussions in Lithuania. They were followed on 11 January by President Gorbachev himself, who took a conciliatory line while making it clear that separatism threatened his reform programme. On a walkabout among ordinary Lithuanians, Gorbachev promised that 'Nothing will be decided without you. We shall decide everything together.' He also stated that a Soviet law was being prepared that would lay down exactly how a republic could secede from the USSR. The Lithuanians, however, seemed unwilling to be bound by Soviet law or to accept delays of any kind.

President Gorbachev (right) arrives in Lithuania.

BLOODSHED IN THE SOUTH

ALMOST simultaneously, disturbances in the southern republic of Azerbaijan assumed a new seriousness, costing at least 200 lives. Ethnic and religious differences between the Azeris of Azerbaijan and their Armenian neighbours had been aggravated since 1988 by disputes over control of Nagorny Karabakh, an Armenian enclave within Azerbaijan; the Soviet government's attempts to keep the peace had pleased neither side. Matters came to a head in mid-January, when Armenians living in Azerbaijan were hunted down by nationalist mobs; many thousands fled from their homes and were evacuated by the Soviet authorities. In some border areas civil war conditions prevailed, with both sides using weapons and armoured vehicles purloined from the Soviet army. After a state of emergency had been declared it was the army that finally restored order, although this involved further bloodshed and led to threats by the Azerbaijan parliament (Supreme Soviet) to secede from the USSR. The capital, Baku, was captured by assault after tanks smashed down street barricades, and artillery was used to destroy ships blockading the city's harbour.

in turmoil

EASTERN EUROPE

ETHNIC conflicts also complicated the situation in Eastern Europe. In Yugoslavia, the congress of the League of Communists, bringing together the communist parties of the various ethnic groups, broke up in confusion after a Slovene walkout. Violence erupted in the province of Kosovo – part of Serbia but with an Albanian majority – when Albanian demonstrators clashed with riot police; some 30 lives were reported lost.

In Bulgaria, nationalists actually demonstrated against one of the government's liberalizing measures which restored the rights of an unpopular minority, the ethnic Turks and Muslim Bulgars. In a more typical development, the former Bulgarian leader Todor Zhivkov, deposed in November 1989, was arrested and faced charges of corruption and abuse of power.

After the bloody Romanian revolution of December 1989 the situation remained confused, with demonstrations and counter-demonstrations and sometimes contradictory government decisions. However, resistance by the former secret police, the Securitate, came to an end, and the National Salvation Front government stayed in power despite accusations that there were many Communists from the former regime in its ranks.

Rapid change continued in East Germany, where the Communist-led coalition gave way to an all-party government and the date for the first free elections was brought forward from May to March. Meanwhile, despite the imminence of a democratic GDR, 2000 people a day continued to leave for West Germany, probably motivated by the bleak economic prospects in the East. These were confirmed by the austerity programme introduced by Poland's Solidarity-led government, which imposed huge price increases and severe restrictions on wage rises. The former ruling Communist party dissolved itself, splitting into two separate social democratic parties.

NORIEGA SURRENDERS

GENERAL Manuel Noriega, dictator-president of Panama until the US invasion in December 1989, gave himself up to the US military on 3 January. He had taken refuge with the papal mission in Panama City, but his unwilling hosts persuaded him to leave by a combination of argument and intense psychological pressure. Noriega was transferred to a cell in Miami, where he was charged with drug-trafficking, although some commentators questioned whether it was legal – or just – for US courts to try a foreign head of state for crimes allegedly committed outside the country. Moreover the most material evidence – a cache of cocaine discovered in a house used by Noriega – was later found to consist of tamales, a mince-and-maize dish popular in Central America.

American forces surround the Vatican Embassy in which General Noriega had taken refuge.

STORM HAVOC

ON 25 January storms swept over north-west Europe, causing almost a hundred deaths, destroying property and disrupting electricity supplies and transport services. Although the 100-mile-an-hour winds were less devastating in their general effects than during the great storms of October 1987, the loss of life was actually greater; 47 people were known to have died in the United Kingdom alone.

Storm damage brings chaos to London.

'DIRTY TRICKS' IN IRELAND

THE violence in Northern Ireland showed no signs of abating in the New Year. There were a number of deaths including those of two taxi drivers, one Catholic and one Protestant, who were killed in separate incidents. An IRA bomb damaged a police station, and an RUC (Royal Ulster Constabulary) inspector was shot dead at his home. Three men – apparently not terrorists – were killed by soldiers in plain-clothes while robbing a betting shop, giving rise to renewed allegations of a 'shoot to kill' policy on the part of the Army. Following a long publicity campaign by Colin Wallace, the British government announced that it would investigate his 1975 dismissal as an army information officer in the province; for most people, the interest of the case lay in Wallace's descriptions of his work as part of an officially sponsored 'dirty tricks' campaign which deliberately spread false information about the situation in Northern Ireland.

FOOTBALL DISASTER REPORT

ON 29 January Lord Justice Taylor presented his final report on the April 1989 Hillsborough Stadium disaster in which 94 Liverpool fans lost their lives in a lethal crush. Having criticized bad decision-making by South Yorkshire police in an interim report, the Lord Justice now focused on inadequate safety measures and facilities at the Sheffield Wednesday ground where the disaster occurred.

CURBS ON UK CATTLE

ALARMED by the outbreak of a fatal brain disease affecting British cattle, agricultural ministers of the European Community imposed restrictions on the import from the UK of live beasts over six months old. Widely known in Britain as 'mad cow disease', bovine spongiform encephalopathy (BSE) gave the brains of its victims a characteristic spongy appearance.

US DEFENCE CUTS

IN the annual State of the Union Address to Congress on 31 January, US President George Bush declared that 'the revolution of 1989' in the Soviet bloc marked 'the beginning of a new era in the world's affairs'. Although predicting that US troops would always be needed in Europe, he proposed that the USA and USSR should each reduce their foces in Central and Eastern Europe to 195,000. Two days earlier, the US budget envisaged defence cuts including the closure of 35 military bases at home and 13 overseas; among those named was Greenham Common, during the 1980s the focus for protests against the installation of Cruise missiles and the site of a woman's 'peace camp'.

HONG KONG APPREHENSIVE

A VISIT to Hong Kong by the British foreign secretary, Douglas Hurd, failed to lay to rest the colony's fears about its future. Leased by the British in 1898, Hong Kong was due to be handed back to China in 1997; and although China's Communist government had agreed to give it a special status, the inhibitants remained unimpressed by promises of democratic self-government. Nor were Hong Kong's three million British passport holders pleased by the British government's plans for citizenship to be available only to a limited number (about 250,000).

Hurd also visited a Vietnamese refugee camp in Hong Kong. With as many as 44,000 Vietnamese 'boat people' detained in compounds as illegal immigrants, the British government proposed to send back those whom it judged to have come in search of better economic opportunities; only those who were thought likely to be victimized for political reasons in Vietnam would be allowed to stay. However, at a United Nations committee meeting this involuntary (enforced) repatriation was vetoed by the USA and Vietnam. It remained in question whether improved schemes to encourage voluntary repatriation would bear fruit.

KASHMIRI CRISIS

FROM December 1989 there were strikes and riots in Kashmir, led by the Kashmir Liberation Front (KLF); the authorities responded by imposing emergency rule and bringing in thousands of Indian troops. The fundamental problem stemmed from the 1947 partition of British-ruled India into two independent states, Muslim Pakistan and a predominantly Hindu India. The majority of the population of Kashmir were Muslims, but its Hindu ruler handed it over to India; and after three Indian-Pakistani wars, India remained in possession of most of this large northern province. As a result of the unrest in Kashmir, relations between India and Pakistan worsened. Pakistan denied that it had helped the KLF, but called for the holding of a plebiscite, supervised by the United Nations, in which the people of Kashmir could vote to decide their own future – a proposal that India had always so far rejected.

IN BRIEF ...

■ In Britain, Norman Fowler resigned as Secretary for Employment; his post, carrying a seat in the cabinet, was taken over by Michael Howard.

■ The first issue of the newspaper *The Independent on Sunday* appeared in Britain on 28 January.

■ European Community foreign ministers met in Dublin and agreed to send emergency food aid to Poland and post-revolutionary Romania.

■ More than 300 people were killed on 4 January in a train collision at Sangi station, Pakistan.

■ In Beijing, the capital of China, martial law was lifted; it had been in force since May 1989, even before the June massacre of pro-democracy demonstrators in Tiananmen Square.

■ The USA's first black state governor, Douglas Wilder, was sworn in at Richmond, Virginia, on 13 January.

■ On 25 January a Boeing 707 belonging to the Colombian national airline crashed on attempting to land at New York's John F. Kennedy airport; 67 died, and only a handful of the 158 people on board escaped uninjured.

Nelson

DE KLERK'S SPEECH

IN his speech on 2 February at the state opening of the South African Parliament, President F.W. de Klerk announced that 71-year-old Nelson Mandela, leader of the banned African National Congress (ANC), was about to be released from prison, Rumours to this effect had circulated for some time, and it had become clear that the ruling Nationalist Party was changing some of its attitudes in the face of continuing international hostility to its system of Apartheid, which in practice maintained white supremacy in South Africa.

However, de Klerk went on to outline an unexpected list of changes. The ban on the ANC, the Pan Africanist Congress (PAC) and the Communist Party was to be lifted. All those imprisoned for membership of these organizations would be released. Many restrictions on reporting and civil rights, imposed under the State of Emergency regulations, would be removed. Death sentences on political activists would not be carried out while new proposals for legal reforms were considered. And talks with black leaders would be sought with a view to framing a new constitution for South Africa.

Nelson Mandela speaks in Soweto after his release.

MANDELA'S VIEWS

BLACK leaders' responses to de Klerk's statement were mixed, for although it represented a long step forward, the State of Emergency remained in force and the main structure of Apartheid was untouched. On the other hand de Klerk was faced by a growing challenge from the Conservative Party, which opposed all concessions to South Africa's black majority, So his gradualist approach was understandable.

Nelson Mandela left the Victor Verster prison in Cape Province on 11 February,

after 27 years of captivity. Celebrations were held all over South Africa and in many other parts of the world, since people of all races had agitated for his release over a long period of years. Mandela, now a spare, grey-haired figure, praised de Klerk as 'a man of integrity' but argued that it was too early for the ANC to renounce armed struggle. Despite his long incarceration he undertook a gruelling programme of speechmaking and interviews, trying in particular to end the bloody confrontations between rival black factions. Then on 27 February he left South Africa to visit supporters and political leaders abroad.

PEACE PROCESS CONTINUES

THE Soviet Union and the United States agreed that each would reduce the number of its troops in Central and Eastern Europe to 195,000. The United States would be allowed to station another 30,000 in other, less sensitive areas such as Great Britain. At almost the same time, NATO and the Warsaw Pact powers agreed on an 'Open Skies' policy whereby unarmed reconnaissance aircraft belonging to one bloc could fly at will over the territory of the other.

Mandela freed

SANDINISTAS DEFEATED IN NICARAGUA

IN the first free elections in Nicaragua for several decades, the ruling Sandinista National Liberation Front suffered an unexpected defeat. After overthrowing the dictator Anastasio Somoza in 1979, the Sandinistas had carried out a programme of radical reforms that had greatly antagonized the United States. The consequent US trade embargo, together with US backing for the Contra guerrillas hoping to overthrow the regime, kept Nicaragua on a permanent battle footing and severely damaged her economy. Nevertheless, when a ceasefire and general amnesty made free elections possible, polls strongly favoured the Sandinistas to win. In the presidential contest that followed, 55 per cent of electors voted for the opposition candidate, Violetta Barrias de Chamorro, and only 40 per cent for the Sandinista leader and incumbent president, Daniel Ortega. Chamorro's National Opposition Union – a potentially fragile alliance of parties ranging from far right to far left – also won a majority in the National Assembly. The many foreign observers in Nicaragua, including a United Nations team, agreed that the Sandinistas had conducted the elections fairly and accepted their defeat without bitterness; and remarks made by the new president suggested that she too wished to heal the wounds of the past and create a degree of national unity. In the United States, President Bush expressed his satisfaction with the result and indicated that the embargo would be lifted. It remained to be seen whether, with US aid, the new government could halt the deterioration of Nicaragua's economy, and how far it would go in dismantling the state created by the Sandinistas.

Waiting to vote in Nicaragua.

ODD WOMAN OUT?

THE European Community took some measures to encourage de Klerk's government on its new course, but argued that the State of Emergency must end before the lifting of sanctions – limits on economic contacts with South Africa – should be considered. This was also Mandela's view. Only Britain disagreed. The British prime minister, Mrs Thatcher, had often argued that sanctions would not work: now, defying her Community colleagues, she announced that new investment in South Africa and the promotion of tourism would no longer be forbidden.

The ban was formally lifted on 23 February, which was also the day when a 'rebel' team of English cricketers flew home. Captained by Mike Gatting, they had ignored the international sporting boycott on South Africa and had agreed to play in the country; but hostile demonstrations persuaded them to cut short their tour.

AMBULANCE WORKERS GO BACK

THE dispute between the ambulance workers and the management of Britain's National Health Service ended on 23 February. A phased pay increase was agreed, said to represent 13.3 per cent over two years. But the union failed to achieve one of its aims – a formula that would automatically set future levels of pay, for example by linking them with the pay of comparable services (police and fire). So the outcome was by no means a clear-cut victory for the ambulance men.

UK AND ARGENTINA: RELATIONS RESUMED

ARGENTINA and the United Kingdom agreed to restore full diplomatic relations between the two countries, broken off in April 1982, at the beginning of the Falklands War. The war was brought about by an Argentinian invasion and occupation of the Falkland Islands, a British colony claimed by Argentina; after some heavy fighting a British task force reoccupied the islands. The new agreement meant that ambassadors would be exchanged, and it also arranged for co-operation in a number of spheres. The Argentinians did not abandon their claim to the Falklands (for which their name was the Malvinas), but were committed to pursue it by peaceful means.

SHARON QUITS

ISRAEL'S minister of trade and industry, Ariel Sharon, resigned. The controversial ultra-right-wing former defence minister denounced government policy towards the Palestinians as insufficiently firm, an opinion rarely voiced outside Israel.

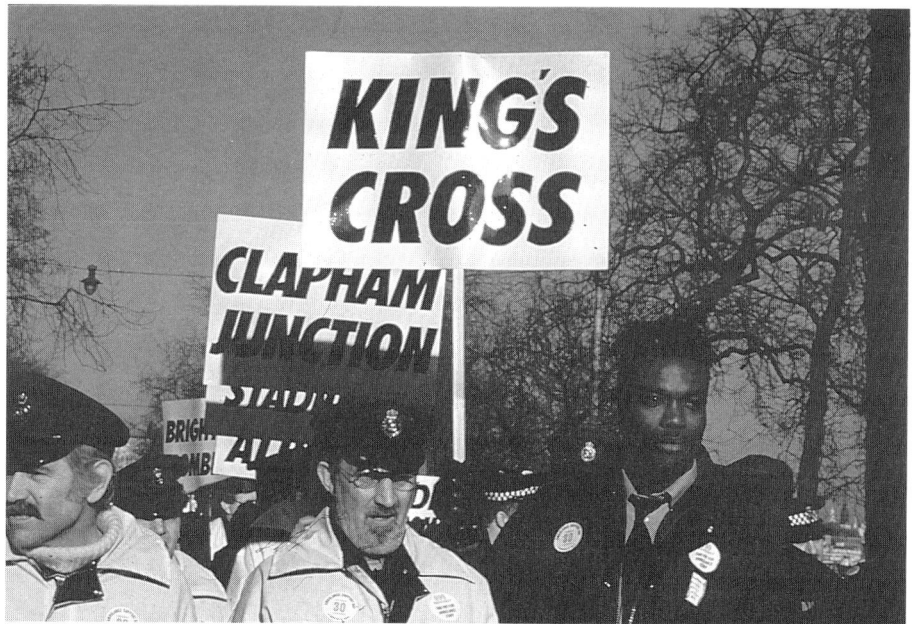

Ambulancemen on the march during their pay dispute.

CHUNNEL TROUBLE

SOARING estimates of the cost of the Channel Tunnel between Britain and France led to public bickering between the financing company, Eurotunnel, and the construction companies. The 1987 estimate of £4870 million was now replaced by a figure of £7200 million.

LEUKAEMIA LINKED TO 'NUKES'

THE Medical Research Council issued a report indicating that the exposure to radiation of workers at the Sellafield nuclear reprocessing plant in Cumbria might have been a cause of leukaemia in their children. Before this, it had often been suggested that there might be a link between unusually concentrated 'clusters' of leukaemia in areas close to nuclear plants: now this seemed highly likely.

HOUSE-BUYERS HURT AGAIN

THE rate of interest on British mortgages (loans made to people buying a house) rose from 14.5 to 15.4 per cent. This was the latest in a series of interest rate increases, brought about by a government policy which aimed to slow down spending by consumers, and so to bring down the rate of inflation (rising prices).

DUBIOUS CONVICTION QUASHED

IN Britain, the Court of Appeal quashed a sentence of 15 years imprisonment, imposed on a man in December 1988 on the basis of a confession extracted from him by West Midlands police. Irregularities, including involuntary confessions, had earlier (14 August 1989) led to the disbanding of the West Midlands Serious Crimes Squad.

JAPAN KEEPS TO THE RIGHT

DESPITE a series of damaging financial scandals, the Japanese general election was again won by the right-wing Liberal Democratic Party, which had ruled the country ever since 1955. Toshiki Kaifu remained in office as prime minister.

Takado Doi, Leader of the Japanese Socialist Party, on the hustings during the 1990 election.

ROMANIA'S NEW GOVERNMENT

AS new political groupings emerged in the aftermath of Romania's December 1989 revolution, a Council of National Unity (CNU) was set up to run the country until its first free elections could be held in May 1990. Thirty-seven political parties and a number of other organizations were represented on the CNU. But the National Salvation Front (NSF), which had run the country since the revolution, dominated the CNU with 112 of the 253 seats, despite accusations that it was merely the former ruling Communist Party under a new name. The NSU president, Ion Ilescu, was appointed president of the CNU executive.

RUSHDIE STILL UNDER SENTENCE

IRAN'S leader, the Ayatollah Khomenei, confirmed the sentence of death passed a year earlier on the British author Salman Rushdie, whose 1988 novel *The Satanic Verses* included a sceptical account of the life of Muhammad, prophet of Islam. The expulsion from Britain of nine Iranians further embittered Anglo-Iranian relations.

DISAPPOINTING EXIT FOR COE

DUE to make the final appearance of his career at the Commonwealth Games held in Auckland, New Zealand, 38-year-old former Olympic gold medallist Sebastion Coe was forced to withdraw because of a viral infection. The race was won by fellow-British runner Peter Elliot.

PARLIAMENT LOOKS INTO 'DIRTY TRICKS'

FOLLOWING the re-emergence of the Colin Wallace affair in January, and complaints about the limited scope of the government's promised enquiry, the House of Commons select committee on defence decided to hold its own investigation.

LEBANON: A PAUSE IN THE FIGHTING

HEAVY fighting between rival Christian groups continued into February, causing widespread destruction in and around Beirut. General Aoun's better-armed forces made only limited gains in their offensive against the LF militia, and on 17 February a ceasefire left the conflict unresolved.

IN BRIEF . . .

■ In a major policy shift. East German prime minister Hans Modrow announced proposals for a four-stage unification of Germany.

■ In Moscow on 4 February a crowd of about 150,000 marched to demonstrate its support for reform.

■ Ninety-two passengers were killed when an Indian Airlines Airbus crashed while attempting to land at Bangalore airport (India).

■ Unrest in Kashmir diminished slightly, but the situation remained tense. A pro-democracy campaign in Nepal faced harsh reactions from the government and police.

■ In Eritrea, the capture of the port of Massawa by soldiers of the Eritrean People's Liberation Front represented an important victory in their struggle for independence from Ethiopia.

■ In Mexico City the government negotiated a debt reduction agreement with its 450 principal creditors.

■ At Cartagena (Colombia) the presidents of the United States, Colombia, Peru and Bolivia agreed to intensify their efforts to suppress cocaine production and the trade in the drug.

Mrs Thatcher's

POLL TAX FURORE

ALREADY facing economic difficulties and domestic unpopularity, Mrs Thatcher's Conservative government was further embarrassed by nationwide protests against the new Poll Tax which was to come into effect in England and Wales on 1 April. This was a local tax introduced to replace the antiquated and admittedly unsatisfactory system of 'rates' which had been levied on households rather than individuals, and had varied according to the supposed value of the house in question. By contrast, the principle of the new tax was that, apart from specified exceptions, everybody within a local authority area should pay the same amount, to be determined by the authority; an authority that spent a great deal on services – whether it was because the services were needed or because they were inefficiently organized – would have to levy a visibly higher rate than low-spending authorities.

Defenders of the new tax claimed that it would encourage the public to monitor local spending, whereas its critics denounced the unfairness of making rich and poor pay the same; it was also hard to collect, as events in Scotland (where it was

Poll Tax demonstrators clash with police in Trafalfar Square on 31 March.

introduced in 1989) had already demonstrated. In practice the Poll Tax was bound to be unpopular, since most people faced substantially higher bills than under the rating system, and in one city after another there were often violent scenes outside and inside council chambers as the local rate was set; even staunch Conservative areas were affected, and there were a number of resignations by Conservative councillors. The culmination of the disturbances occurred at a demonstration in London, called by the Anti-Poll Tax Federation on 31 March, at which there were several hundred arrests.

BY-ELECTION SHOCK

AT the Mid-Staffordshire by-election on 22 March, the Labour candidate, Sylvia Heal, overturned a 14,654 majority and won the seat by a margin of 9449. The swing to Labour of 21 per cent was the largest in any election since 1935, reflecting public resentment of the Poll Tax and the high interest rates which, among other things, made mortgages cripplingly expensive for house-buyers.

MILD BUDGET

JOHN MAJOR'S first budget as Chancellor of the Exchequer was unexpectedly cautious. It gave some encouragement to savers, but fears that there might be cuts in tax allowances and other stringent measures proved groundless. Despite the absence of encouraging signs the Chancellor appeared content to rely on already high interest rates to curb runaway consumer spending and the inflation (rising prices) resulting from it.

NORTH SEA DEBATE

MEETING at the Hague, the North Sea Conference agreed on drastic reductions in the amounts of pollutants being released into the sea. The United Kingdom was generally regarded as being behindhand in ending the dumping of industrial waste and sewage; and Chris Patten, Secretary of State for the Environment, angered the conference by refusing to renounce the possibility of disposing of radioactive waste beneath the sea bed.

JOURNALIST EXECUTED

DESPITE pleas for clemency from Britain and the international community, on 15 March the journalist Farzad Bazoft was hanged as a spy in Iraq. His offence was to have made an unauthorized visit to the Al-Iskandria weapons plant, where a devastating explosion, costing hundreds of lives, was reported to have occurred; Daphne Parish, a British nurse who drove Bazoft to the site, was sentenced to 15 years' imprisonment. Although Iranian-born, the 31-year-old Bazoft had British travel documents and was working for the *Observer* newspaper; many commentators assumed that his motives were purely journalistic, but the Iraqi authorities insisted that he had been spying for Israel.

The British prime minister, Mrs Thatcher, condemned the execution as 'an act of barbarism', but authorized only minor reprisals. However, British-Iraqi relations became even worse after 40 devices, said to be nuclear detonators, were confiscated at Heathrow airport on their way to Iraq, which claimed that they were harmless electrical capacitors intended for use with air-conditioning equipment.

SOVIET CHANGES

IN Moscow, the Congress of People's Deputies endorsed the creation of a new, much stronger 'executive' presidency, and elected Mikhail Gorbachev as the first incumbent. The effect of this change was to strengthen the state at the expense of the Communist Party, which also lost the political monopoly guaranteed to it by the constitution. The changes aroused opposition among delegates who feared that a president with such wide powers might become a virtual dictator, although Gorbachev's declared motive was to speed up his programme of *perestroika* – the reconstruction of Soviet society and the economy.

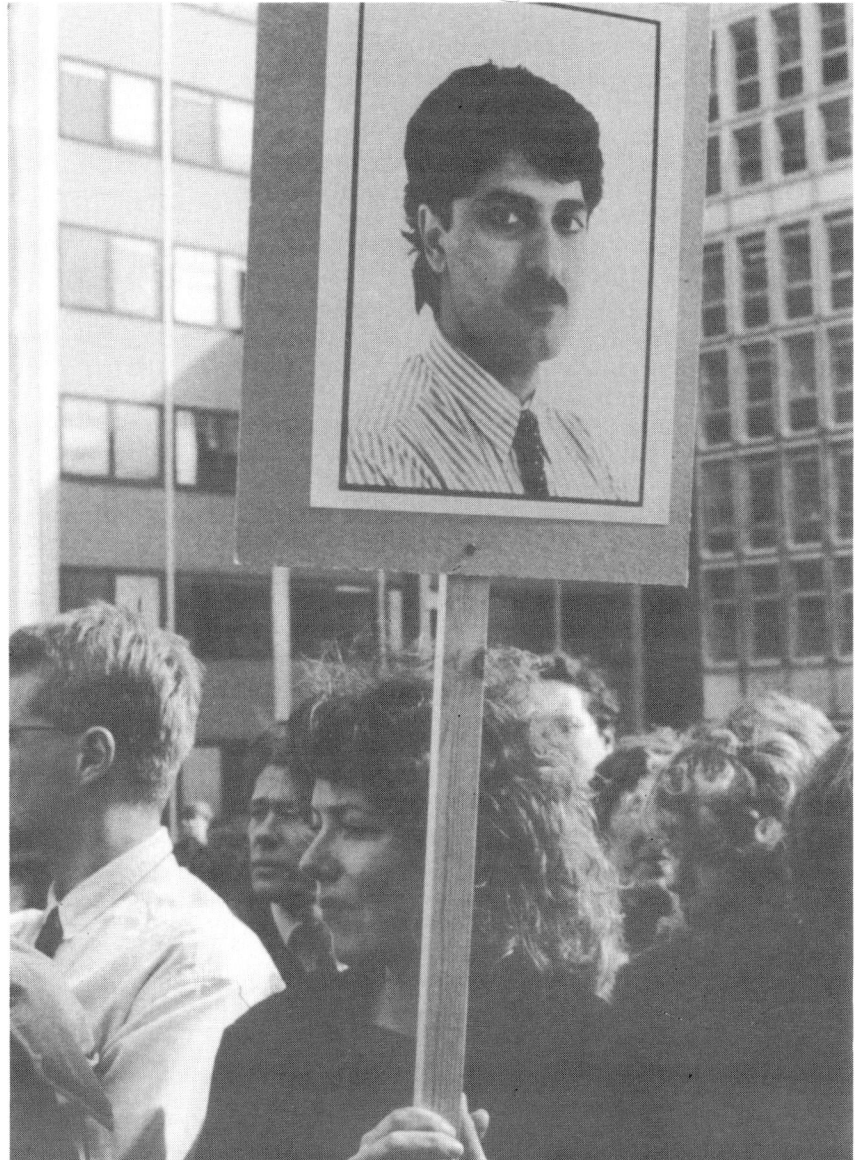

Demonstrators in London protest at the execution of journalist Farzad Bazoft.

EXIT LITHUANIA?

MEANWHILE elections in most parts of the the USSR brought sweeping radical victories in big cities such as Moscow and Leningrad, and confirmed the strong nationalist trend in the Baltic republics. Lithuania continued to adopt the boldest course, despite Gorbachev's conciliatory visit to the republic in January. A non-communist, Vytautas Landsbergis, was elected president, Lithuania declared its independence, and the Soviet hammer-and-sickle emblem was removed from the flag and taken down from public buildings in the republic. In response, President Gorbachev declared the Lithuanian action illegal and, with Soviet troops still on Lithuanian soil, a tense situation developed.

President Patricio Aylwin (left) accepts power in Chile, ending almost 17 years of military rule by General Augusto Pinochet (second from right).

DEBT REDUCED

AN agreement was reached between Venezuala and 400 banks to reduce and reorganize the country's debts. This was the latest in a series of efforts to tackle a fearful problem – basically that the poor countries of the "Third World" owed so much that many of them were struggling to keep up interest payments on their loans, without having the slightest prospect of ever paying off the principal.

ISRAELI COALITION COLLAPSES

DISAGREEMENTS over a US-sponsored Middle Eastern peace plan caused Israel's Labour Party, which favoured rapid adoption of the plan, to leave the coalition government of Yitzhak Shamir and defeat it on a vote of no confidence. But the Labour leader, Shimon Peres, failed to form a new government and Shamir remained in office as caretaker prime minister.

SCARGILL ACCUSED

SERIOUS allegations were made in the *Daily Mirror* newspaper and on television against the president of the National Union of Mineworkers (NUM), Arthur Scargill. During the coalminers' national strike in 1984-85 Scargill was said to have received funds from Libya and the Soviet Union which were grossly misused. The NUM decided to set up an independent inquiry into the allegations.

GDR ELECTIONS

THE first free elections in East Germany (the German Democratic Republic) were won by the Christian Democrats (CDU) and their allies, who polled 48 per cent of the votes cast. The Social Democrats, who had been widely expected to do well, polled just under 22 per cent. Both parties had massive help from their counterparts in West Germany, and New Forum and other radical groups largely responsible for the democratization of East Germany made no impact. The former ruling Communist Party (Socialist Unity Party) took part under a new name, the Party of Democratic Socialism, and won a respectable 16 per cent of the votes. The victory of the CDU represented a mandate for rapid monetary and political union of the two Germanies.

JUSTICE DENIED?

DOUBTS continued to surface concerning the 1975 conviction of the 'Birmingham Six' for two horrific pub bombings in 1974. Although the Court of Appeal had confirmed the verdict in January 1988, on 21 March 1990 Home Secretary David Waddington announced that there would be a new inquiry by Devon and Cornwall police. A week later, a television programme, Granada World in Action, went so far as to name four people whom it alleged to be responsible for the bombings. Also damaging to the reputation of British justice was a decision by the Irish Supreme Court, which refused to extradite two IRA men who had escaped from Northern Ireland's Maze prison; probably influenced by successful legal actions brought by former Maze inmates, the court based its decision on the likelihood of the escapees being maltreated by prison staff.

NAMBIA INDEPENDENT

ON 21 March a new nation was born. Namibia, which had long been ruled by South Africa in defiance of the United Nations, became an independent south-west African state with Sam Nujoma as its first president. Nujoma was the leader of SWAPO (the South West African People's Organization), which had fought for independence since 1960 and had won the elections held under UN supervision in November 1989.

LIBYAN FIRE

A FIRE at Libya's Rabta chemical plant on 15 March was followed by government accusations that agents employed by Israel, the United States and/or West Germany had been responsible. The plant had been persistently criticized by the US, which claimed that it was being used to manufacture chemical weapons, whereas the Libyan leader, Colonel Gadaffi, insisted that only pharmaceutical goods were produced there. In view of the long-standing hostility between Libya and the United States, the truth of these claims and counter-claims was hard to determine.

IN BRIEF . . .

■ An extraordinary congress of Italy's powerful communist party voted to change its title and restructure it as a social democratic party open to a wider spectrum of left-wing views.

■ After fierce fighting in Kabul, the capital of Afghanistan, an attempted army coup led by the defence minister was foiled.

■ A revolt against the Philippines government of Cory Aquino was crushed.

■ In the Australian general election the Labour Party was returned to power, although with a reduced majority, and Bob Hawke began a record fourth term as premier.

■ In Zimbabwe, President Robert Mugabe and his ZANU-PF party retained power in elections notable for popular apathy.

■ Newly released from prison, Nelson Mandela was elected deputy president of the African National Congress; he later had an emotional meeting in Sweden with the ANC president, Oliver Tambo, who was recovering from a stroke.

■ Ciskei dictator Lennox Sebe was overthrown, and there were disturbances in other black South African 'homelands' (puppet mini-states set up by the white South African government).

■ General Prosper Avril, dictator of Haiti, was forced to resign and leave the country, which he had ruled since October 1988.

■ 87 people died in a fire at a New York social club; later a man was charged with arson.

■ After almost 17 years of military rule in Chile by General Augusto Pinochet, a democratically elected president, Patricio Aylwin, was sworn in on 11 March.

The Supergun

THE SUPERGUN AFFAIR

IRAQ'S arms build-up continued to make news. Following the interception in March of alleged nuclear triggers, on 10 April British customs officers at Middlesborough's Teesport dock prevented the export to Iraq of pipes that were said to be components of a huge 'supergun'. The Iraqi authorities denied this, claiming that the parts were for use in the country's petro-chemical industry. Public concern over the issue was partly diverted by media coverage of the plight of a British lorry driver, held for three weeks in Greece because his vehicle was carrying a consignment of the illicit materials.

Although charges were brought against some executives, the role played by British firms in illegally exporting such military equipment was unclear, since a Conservative MP, Sir Hilary Miller, claimed that he had passed on the firms' suspicions concerning the true purpose of the parts to the Department of Trade and Industry and the Ministry of Defence. Subsequent investigations showed that Iraq's already formidable forces – easily the strongest of any Arab state – were being supplied through a complicated network of dealers and 'front' companies. A Brussels company, the Space Research Organization (SRO), was reported to have designed a large-calibre gun for

Parts for the Iraqi 'supergun' discovered by the Greek authorities after the British lorry transporting it was stopped for examination.

Iraq, and the assassination in March of SRO's owner, Canadian Gerald Bull, now seemed typical of the murky world of the international arms trade.

The strained nature of Western-Iraqi relations also appeared in the American expulsion of an Iraqi diplomat who was said to have been implicated in plots to murder exiled fellow-countrymen in the USA who were hostile to the current regime. Nevertheless, it was assumed that if Iraq had any aggressive intentions they would be directed towards Israel. For his part, Iraq's president, Saddam Hussein, asserted that the West and Israel were using his country's supposed nuclear build-up as an excuse for an imminent Israeli attack. He declared that Iraq's chemical weapons would prove as effective as atom bombs, for 'by God we will make the fire eat up half of Israel if it tries to do anything against Iraq'.

LITHUANIA UNDER SIEGE

AS Lithuania steadfastly refused to withdraw its declaration of independence, the USSR took an increasingly strong line. Properties previously belonging to the central authorities in Moscow – including nuclear power stations and the Communist Party headquarters in Vilnius – were occupied by Soviet troops; Lithuanian deserters from the Red Army were rounded up; and on 18 April an economic blockade was declared. Meanwhile a Soviet law was passed which allowed any republic to leave the USSR after a five-year transition period if two-thirds of its citizens approved.

Since Lithuania was heavily dependent on subsidized Soviet fuel and raw materials, the effects of the blockade began to be felt immediately, and rationing was introduced. Western responses to Lithuanian appeals for recognition and help were muted, perhaps because Lithuania's hasty, uncompromising course was seen as undermining USSR President Gorbachev's position at a time when he was trying to overcome opposition to the throughgoing reform and democratization of the entire Soviet Union.

BRITAIN'S PRISON RIOTS

ON 1 April disturbances in the chapel at Manchester's Strangeways prison developed into a full-scale riot and a long-lasting defiance of the authorities. Prisoners occupied most of the establishment and conducted a vocal, well-publicized rooftop protest that went on until the last five men surrendered on 25 April, leaving the prison virtually a ruin. Although hosepipes were sometimes played on the roofs, the reaction of the authorities was generally restrained – too much so for some tastes; later there were disputes over who had taken the decision not to storm the prison. Other observers noted that the episode had passed off without loss of life through direct confrontation, although one man, an alleged sex offender, died as a result of injuries apparently inflicted by other prisoners.

Shorter-lived 'copy-cat' disturbances were sparked off at several institutions including Pucklechurch Remand Centre, where inmates surrendered after an 18-hour siege. Home Office minister David Mellor defended current policy and said that inmates 'took the opportunity to behave badly because that's why most people are in prison'. But many observers placed the blame for the riots on the appalling conditions in Britain's overcrowded prisons.

Aftermath of the riot at Strangeways prison, Manchester.

EASTERN EUROPE

THE dismantling of one-party rule continued apace in Eastern Europe. The decisive second round of the Hungarian elections resulted in a clear victory for the centre-right parties (Hungarian Democratic Forum; Christian Democratic People's Party; Independent Smallholder's Party), which won 229 of the 386 contested seats. In Bulgaria the ruling Bulgarian Communist Party renamed itself the Bulgarian Socialist Party and prepared for free elections in June. Elections in the Yugoslav republics of Slovenia and Crotia favoured strongly nationalist candidates, arousing fears of secession from the federation or ethnic violence. In Czechoslovakia, however, the long-standing argument over the name of the state, which Slovaks interpreted as subordinating them to the Czechs, appeared to have been solved by the adoption of the new title, the Czech and Slovak Federative Republic. And a meeting of Czechoslovak, Hungarian and Polish leaders at Bratislava (Czechoslovakia) foreshadowed a 'return to Europe' in the form of membership of the European Community and similar insitutions.

EAST GERMAN COALITION

DESPITE earlier reservations, East Germany's Social Democrats joined a coalition government led by the Christian Democratic prime minister Lothar de Maizière. Both right and left were therefore represented, although the reformed Communist PDS was excluded. Aiming to achieve monetary and economic union by July, the new government persuaded a reluctant West Germany to concede in most cases a one-to-one conversion of East to West German marks, despite the higher value of the West German currency. Early political unification remained an objective, although difficulties to be overcome included opposition by the Soviet Union to a unified Germany becoming part of the Western military alliance (NATO).

SOVIETS ADMIT MASSACRE

AS part of the process of coming to terms with its Stalinist past, on 13 April the Soviet Union admitted responsibility for a 50-year-old atrocity. In 1943, during the Second World War, German forces invading the USSR discovered thousands of corpses in a mass grave in the Katyn forest. They asserted that these Polish officers had been murdered by the Soviets, who countered by claiming that the corpses were victims of Nazism. Now, according to the Soviet new agency Tass, historians had discovered documents that put the matter beyond question, indicating that some 15,000 officers had been deported from eastern Poland in 1939 and killed at Katyn and other sites.

GLOBAL WARMING: US COOL

AN international conference on global warming, held at the White House, Washington, DC, was viewed by many European delegates as little more than an excuse for a 'lecture' by American president George Bush. Global warming, a phenomenon widely believed to be taking place as a result of rising temperatures, would have disastrous effects, for example in raising sea levels and flooding low-lying countries. A major cause is held to be the 'greenhouse gases' such as carbon dioxide, of which the USA is the world's leading producer. President Bush's view was that much more research was needed before any action should be taken, and that economic disruption through environmental measures must be avoided at all costs. By contrast, West Germany's Minister of the Environment, Klaus Töpfer, gave a typical European response, warning that 'gaps in knowledge must not be used as an excuse for worldwide inaction'.

Grisly evidence of the Katyn massacre, now admitted by the Soviet Union to have been a Stalinist crime.

A UNITED EUROPE?

MEETING at Dublin, leaders of the 12 European Community member states welcomed the prospect of German unification and began to contemplate the possibility of a politically united Europe. A joint Franco-German proposal urged that, with a single European market already on the agenda for 1 January 1993, the Community should aim at political union by the same date. A further conference was envisaged before the end of 1990. Britain's Mrs Thatcher remained hostile to any significant sacrifice of national sovereignty to 'European' institutions, but avoided the appearance of disagreement by stressing that the nature of political union was as yet undefined. 'Clearly they [the French and German leaders] do not know what they mean by it. Political union at the moment means very different things to different people.'

HUBBLE IN PLACE

JOINTLY developed by the US and European space agencies, the 11 tonne Hubble telescope was put into orbit 380 miles above the earth at the beginning of April by the shuttle *Discovery*. The placing of a telescope in space, clear of the Earth's masking atmosphere, promised to bring immeasurable improvements in human understanding of the universe.

NEW ABORTION LAW

IN Britain, the House of Commons voted to restrict the period during which a pregnancy could legally be terminated by abortion: in most circumstances this was to be up to 24 (and no longer 28) weeks after conception.

Pro-democracy demonstrators in Kathmandu.

NEPAL DEMOCRATIZED

EARLY in April the political scene in monarchist Nepal was transformed by a pro-democracy campaign of a kind more familiar in Eastern Europe. Shootings of demonstrators by police failed to halt the momentum of the Movement for the Restoration of Democracy. After demonstrations, strikes and shootings King Birendra gave way to the MRD's demand for the legalization of political parties. A new government was formed by Krishna Prasad Bhattarai of the previously banned Nepali Congress Party, and the way seemed open for elections within the year and the creation of a constitutional monarchy.

'THREE' FREE

THE Court of Appeal quashed 25-year prison sentences on the 'Winchester Three', alleged IRA terrorists convicted of conspiracy to murder the Northern Ireland Secretary, Tom King. During their trial the three defendants had exercised their right to silence. Within hours King had announced that the government intended to curb this right because it led to the acquittal of too many guilty people – a statement that the Court of Appeal held to have hopelessly prejudiced the then-unfinished trial. Subsequently the 'Three' were deported from the UK under an Exclusion Order.

COUNCILS CAPPED

CHRIS PATTEN, the Minister of the Environment, announced that 21 English local authorities would be 'capped' – that is, would have a government-imposed limit placed on the amount of Poll Tax (community charge) that they could raise to pay for local services. Faced with the prospect of severe cutbacks, 20 of the authorities prepared to challenge the ruling in the courts. Already under fire because of the unpopularity of the tax, Patten was now accused of political partisanship, since all 21 capped councils were Labour-controlled while 'high-spending' Conservative authorities were not similarly penalized.

IN BRIEF . . .

- Despite a revolt by 44 Conservative MPs, the House of Commons voted in favour of plans to give 50,000 Hong Kong families the option of becoming British citizens.
- During a two-day visit to Britain, South African black leader Nelson Mandela made a triumphant appearance at a Wembley concert held in his honour.
- Britain's second satellite TV network, British Satellite Broadcasting (BSB), began transmissions.
- Representatives of 112 countries attended a three-day World Ministerial Drugs Conference in London.
- A 21-year-old Scot, Stephen Hendry, became the youngest-ever world snooker champion, beating Jimmy White 18-12 in the final at Sheffield.
- About 159 people perished when a fire broke out on a ferry sailing from Oslo (Norway) to Frederikshavn (Denmark).
- Oskar Lafontaine, leader of West Germany's opposition Social Democratic Party, spent a week in hospital after being stabbed in the neck by 42-year-old woman with a history of mental illness.
- In the third Greek election within a year, the right-wing New Democracy party won exactly half the 300 parliamentary seats, and was able to form a government.
- Five hostages – French, Belgian and American – were released by revolutionary groups in the Lebanese capital, Beirut.
- A small-scale Muslim rebellion was reported to have been suppressed in the Chinese province of Xinjiang.
- Morocco's debts to commercial banks were rescheduled, and the rates of interest on them lowered.
- Nigeria's military government survived a coup attempt by Major Orkar and other dissatisfied officers.
- In Gabon, Omar Bongo, president since 1967, yielded to demands for the immediate introduction of a multi-party system.
- In Colombia, an assassin shot dead Carlos Pizarro, the presidential candidate of the newly formed left-alliance group, Democratic Convergence.

PROTEST AND PANIC

EVENTS in May highlighted the multiple problems of the Soviet leadership, beginning with the disruption of the traditional May Day celebrations in Moscow by thousands of anti-Gorbachev demonstrators, whose heckling drove the President and his party from the balcony on which they were watching the parade. The incident – unthinkable at any time in the previous seventy years – revealed the new freedom of expression, and also the unresolved tensions, in the USSR.

Plans to restore the deteriorating Soviet economy also ran into trouble when it became obvious that they entailed drastic price rises. There was much hostile public reaction, and a wave of panic buying only made existing shortages worse.

Lithuanian prime minister Kazimiera Prunskiene with US president George Bush.

RUSSIA VS SOVIETS?

ALMOST simultaneously, Gorbachev's principal rival, Boris Yeltsin, became effective president of the Russian Federation (RSFSR), by far the largest and most powerful of the republics making up the USSR. After lengthy political manoeuvres during which Gorbachev was believed to have openly worked against him, Yeltsin was narrowly elected by the Congress of People's Deputies, polling 535 votes to the 467 of Alexander Vlasov. Although presenting himself as a radical economic reformer, Yeltsin declared that 'We will have to find a way of going over to a market economy without sharp price increases.' How these seemingly incompatible aims could be achieved was not clear. He also called for a degree of political and economic sovereignty for the RSFSR that seemed likely to undermine Gorbachev's authority and threaten the already shaky unity of the USSR.

Gorbachev, visiting Ottowa, reacted to the news of Yeltsin's victory with obvious concern, expressing the hope that they could work together but commenting that 'If he is playing political games, then perhaps we are in for a difficult time.' Yeltsin responded with a characteristic mixture of conciliatory and belligerent remarks that left the issue in doubt.

Demonstrators disrupt the traditional May Day parade in Red Square.

BALTIC DEADLOCK

MEANWHILE Latvia followed the example of Lithuania and Estonia in proclaiming its independence from the USSR, and the three countries revived the pre-war Baltic Council to co-ordinate their tactics. However, Latvia, like Estonia, took a cautious line, effectively suspending its declaration of independence and anticipating a transitional period and negotiations before it became a reality. By contrast, Lithuania's more uncompromising policy meant that the Soviet economic blockade remained in force and began to bite. The Lithuanian prime minister, Kazimiera Prunskiene, toured abroad, winning sympathy but little practical help. Towards the end of the month there were indications that both sides were ready to negotiate, although Lithuanian reluctance even to suspend its declaration of independence remained an obstacle.

ELECTIONS IN THREE CONTINENTS

THERE were several important elections in May. In Romania the victor was the National Salvation Front, which had run the country since the overthrow of the Ceausescu dictatorship in December 1989. The NSF and its presidential candidate, Ion Iliescu, won a commanding majority in a contest which was recognized by observers as marred by irregularities but basically fair. The presence of many former Communists in the NSF was widely commented on, and the election result was the first in Eastern Europe not characterized by a sharp swing to the right.

The most unexpected result occurred in Myanma (Burma), where the elections held by the military government had been intended as a sham, held to placate

Ion Iliescu, Rumania's new democratically elected president.

Western critics in view of the country's urgent need of foreign investment. But in spite of the arrest of opponents, censorship and other forms of government repression, the opposition National League for Democracy won an overwhelming victory. It remained to be seen whether its control of a Constituent Assembly with very limited powers would bring about a more democratic system.

Other results were more predictable. The Colombian presidential elections were won by César Gaviria Trujillo of the ruling Liberal Party, who promised to maintain the offensive against the drug cartels. In Italy regional elections left the parties in much the same position as before, although the Communist Party, in the throes of transforming itself into a social-democratic-style party, lost some ground. And local elections in Britain led

to the expected Labour gains from both the Conservatives and the Liberal Democrats, although the government took some comfort from Conservative successes in holding the London boroughs of Wandsworth and Westminster, where council policy had led to the setting of a low Poll Tax.

GRAVES DESECRATED

IN France, damage and disfigurement of Jewish graves at Carpentras and elsewhere renewed fears of a resurgence of anti-semitism and other forms of racism. The far-right National Front was widely blamed for its part in stimulating hostility towards minorities and immigrants; its leader, Jean-Marie Le Pen, reacted by denouncing the incident as 'a fake', designed to discredit his party. On 14 May thousands of people, including the President and Prime Minister of France, took part in a silent anti-racist march through Paris.

2+4 MEET

THE first round of 'two-plus-four' talks at Bonn, West Germany, brought together the foreign ministers of four Second World War allies (USA, Britain, USSR, France) and the two (West and East) Germanies. The 'four' had been the occupying powers at the close of the war, and still retained treaty rights that gave them a say in German affairs. With the unification process accelerating, the main stumbling block appeared to be the future relationship between the new Germany and the NATO western military alliance, which constituted a source of anxiety to the Soviet Union.

BENSONHURST VERDICT

AT a time when tensions between ethnic groups in New York City were particularly acute, the outcome of a murder trial was seen as critically important. In August 1989 a young black who entered the predominantly Italian Bensonhurst neighbourhood of Brooklyn was set upon by a mob and shot dead; two youths, believed to be the ringleaders, were charged with murder. Black indignation was sustained – and, some felt, exploited – by the black Baptist minister Al Sharpton, who voiced fears that racial prejudice would prevent justice from being done; and hostility between blacks and Koreans further raised the emotional temperature. The verdicts of the court were apparently contradictory, since one of the accused was found guilty of murder while the other – generally considered more obviously culpable – was convicted only on lesser charges. However, severe sentencing helped to defuse the situation. David Dinkins, New York's first black mayor, behaved with a studied moderation that was not appreciated on all sides.

Racial tension in New York – blacks demonstrate outside a Korean grocery store.

The intifada continues – a pro-PLO demonstration by Arabs in Israel.

INTIFADA GOES ON

THE murder of seven Palestinians by an apparently unhinged Israeli gave renewed impetus to the Arab *intifada* or 'uprising' (really widespread disturbances rather than an armed revolt) in Israel's Occupied Territories. Although Israeli President Chaim Herzog declared that the incident was 'a loathsome crime against innocent Arabs', more lives were lost as a result of riots, shootings by the Israeli army, and a bomb attack by the Islamic Jihad group. In the West, sympathy for the Palestine Liberation Organization (PLO), which had in recent times adopted a moderate line, was weakened after 30 May, when the affiliated Palestine Liberation Front launched an unsuccessful guerrilla assault on Israeli beaches crowded with civilians.

RAINBOW'S END

A GLIMPSE of the dark underside of diplomacy was offered by the former New Zealand prime minister David Lange, who claimed that in 1986 the French government had virtually blackmailed him into releasing two of its agents. They had been given prison sentences for causing explosions in Auckland harbour that sank the *Rainbow Warrior* and killed a photographer; the vessel belonged to the Greenpeace environmental group and was scheduled to lead protests against French nuclear tests in the Pacific. According to Lange, his government agreed to release the men into French custody in the face of threats to close French markets to New Zealand's vital agricultural exports. Lange's statement coincided with a UN arbitration panel's ruling that France had subsequently broken the terms of this agreement by repatriating the agents.

LOCKERBIE REPORT

RADICAL recommendations were made in a report on the Lockerbie disaster of December 1988, when a Pan Am airliner crashed on the Scottish town after a terrorist bomb exploded. Issued by a US presidential commission, the report criticized Pan Am's lax security and stirred up controversy by urging the US government to pre-empt (anticipate) or retaliate against such atrocities by direct military action against 'outlaw nations sponsoring terrorism'.

Manchester United captain Bryan Robson holds aloft the FA cup.

CLOSE CUP FINALS

ABERDEEN became Scottish FA cupholders on 12 May after a tense struggle with Celtic at Hampden Park; with no goals scored after extra time, they emerged 9–8 ahead from a penalty shootout.

On the same day, at Wembley, Manchester United and Crystal Palace drew 3–3 in the English final. United won the replay on 17 May by a single goal, scored in the 59th minute by Lee Martin.

YEMENIS UNITE

ON 22 May North and South Yemen merged into a single Republic of Yemen. San'aa, former capital of the (northern) Yemen Arab Republic, became the political capital of the new state, while Aden (capital of the southern People's Democratic Republic) became its commercial and economic capital. Recent events, encouraging the liberalization of Marxist regimes such as South Yemen, undoubtedly made the process of unification smoother.

NEW IRA CAMPAIGN

THE Northern Irish issue continued to cause a monthly toll of deaths, and in May there were indications that the IRA was undertaking a new campaign abroad. At Wembley, London, a soldier was killed when a bomb exploded under a van, and at Roermond in the Netherlands two Australian lawyers were shot dead by an IRA unit which mistook them for British servicemen stationed in Europe.

In Britain itself, a judicial inquiry began into the cases of two groups of people convicted as terrorists, the 'Guildford Four' (released in October 1989) and the 'Maguire Seven'.

BEEF BANNED

THE death of a Siamese cat from symptoms resembling those of 'mad cow disease' – BSE – raised new fears that human beings too might be liable to infection. Most expert British opinion dismissed the danger as negligable, but many local authorities banned the use of native beef (for example in school meals), and at the end of the month France prohibited imports of British beef and cattle.

IN BRIEF . . .

- In Britain, a new weekly, *The European*, was launched to cater to the growing 'Euro-consciousness' of the public.

- David Hunt succeeded Peter Walker as Secretary of State for Wales; Hunt's former post as Minister for Local Government and the Inner Cities was taken by Michael Portillo.

- Former Minister of Defence Michael Heseltine called for substantial changes in the poll tax, an action interpreted (despite his denials) as part of an effort to present himself as an alternative Conservative leader to Mrs Thatcher.

- Continuing an already pronounced trend, British Coal projected that pit closures over the next three years would cost 7500 jobs.

- In Paris, a European Bank for Reconstruction and Development was set up to assist economic change in Eastern Europe.

- There were reports of strikes and disturbances in Albania, the last old-style Communist country in Europe, and citizens were promised new legal rights, including the right to obtain a passport for travel abroad.

- Natural disasters cost many lives, notably in the Indian state of Andra Pradesh, devastated by a cyclone, and in Romanian and Peruvian earthquakes.

- Fresh violence broke out in Kashmir when Indian security police fired on mourners after the murder of a leading Muslim; while Hyderabad and Karachi in Pakistan's Sind province were also the scenes of ethnic strife and police shootings, in this instance between Sind nationals and Muslim Indian immigrants.

- In Cape Town, South Africa, cordial and optimistic talks took place between the African National Congress and government representatives, with a view to clearing the way for formal negotiations.

- The rebel government controlling Bougainville declared the island's independence of Papua New Guinea, which was attempting to regain control by means of an economic blockade.

- In Caracas, the Venezuelan capital, the government of El Salvador and the FMNLF guerrillas tentatively arranged for a ceasefire in mid-September.

Earthquake

EARTHQUAKE DEVASTATES IRAN

ON 21 June, north-west Iran was devastated by a series of shocks that wrecked towns and villages, killed some 40,000 people, injured many thousands more, and left hundreds of thousands homeless. As in other such disasters, there were harrowing scenes as rescuers searched for possible survivors, and medical and other supplies were in short supply. According to one survivor, 'The disaster was of such a horrifying magnitude that in some villages not even a single person survived to bury the dead.' Iran's fundamentalist Islamic government expressed its willingness to accept aid, but even in this crisis laid down various religious and political conditions. Nevertheless aid flowed in from many parts of the world, including countries with whom Iran had no diplomatic relations and her enemy of the Gulf War, Iraq. Consequently it was hoped that happier relations between Iran and the rest of the world might prove to be a by-product of the catastrophe.

Earthquake devastation in Iran.

E. EUROPE VOTES: MINERS STRIKE

FURTHER elections in Eastern Europe revealed an increasing diversity of trends. In Czecho-slovakia, Civic Forum and its Slovak ally, Public Against Violence, won 46 per cent of the votes; the Communist Party, with 13 per cent, became the second largest grouping. A broad coalition rather than a political party, Civic Forum undoubtedly benefited from its role in discrediting the previous regime and its association with the former dissident hero Vaclav Havel, now president of the state.

By contrast, Bulgaria became the only ex-Communist state to re-elect the former ruling party, now renamed the Bulgarian Socialist Party. One reason was believed to be the close ties of sentiment and language that existed between Bulgars and Russians, which meant that anti-Soviet national feeling had relatively little influence on electors.

The most sensational events occurred in Romania, where many thousands of demonstrators had been installed since April in Bucharest's University Square, turning it into a many-tented 'town'. Despite the election victory of the National Salvation Front, the demonstrators remained hostile to it, and police action in clearing the square only prompted a violent reoccupation accompanied by acts of arson and Molotov-cocktail throwing. President-elect Ion Iliescu appealed for help to Romanian miners, some 10,000 of whom entered the square on 14 June, armed with clubs, and went on a two-day rampage in which hundreds were injured and the premises of opposition parties were broken up. Iliescu thanked the miners for their help, but later admitted that excesses had been committed and ordered an inquiry. Western reaction were highly critical of the NSF, and the US Ambassador boycotted the swearing-in of Iliescu as president; some observers, however, noted that the violence had been begun by the protesters, whose attempts to bring down the elected government were scarcely democratic in spirit.

LITHUANIA: CRISIS OVER?

ON 29 June Lithuania yielded to Soviet pressure by suspending its declaration of independence for 100 days, during which negotiations could take place. In return the Soviet government lifted its economic blockade, and life in Lithuania returned to normal. Elsewhere in the USSR, national and ethnic problems continued to loom large, notably in violent clashes between Kirghiz and Uzbeks in Soviet Central Asia.

devastates Iran

NEW ISRAELI GOVERNMENT

WITH neither major party able to command a majority in Israel's parliament, the breakdown of the Likud-Labour coalition was followed by months of negotiations during which each bid for the support of MPs from other, mainly religiously oriented parties. An extended effort by Labour's Shimon Peres failed, dimming hopes of Israeli participation in the US-backed peace plan for the Middle East. The cabinet formed by Yitzhak Shamir (Likud, hitherto 'caretaker' prime minister) was widely described as the most right-wing in Israel's history. It was committed to promoting Jewish settlement on the West Bank and the Gaza Strip in the Occupied Territories, a development widely regarded outside Israel as making peace in the Middle East increasingly remote.

American dismay at the new government's stance was conveyed by US Secretary of State James Baker with some

Israeli prime minister Yitzhak Shamir (third from left) with his new cabinet.

irony as he told the Israelis the White House telephone number and said 'When you're serious about peace, call us!' However, in an apparently contradictory (or even-handed?) move later in the

month, the United States broke off its 'dialogue' with the Palestine Liberation Organization pending a satisfactory response to PLO involvement with terrorist attacks such as the attempted landing on Israeli beaches in May.

WASHINGTON SUMMIT

AT a summit meeting held between 31 May and 3 June in Washington, DC, Presidents Bush and Gorbachev made further progress towards complete Soviet-American reconciliation. Agreements were signed prohibiting the manufacture of chemical weapons, providing a framework for drastic reductions of strategic nuclear arms, and greatly extending trade and cultural contacts. Even more impressive was the clear intention of the two leaders to work towards solutions of outstanding problems that would be acceptable to both.

Presidents Gorbachev and Bush at the Washington summit.

'SEVEN' WRONGFULLY CONVICTED

THE inquiry into the cases of the Guildford Four and Maguire Seven ended abruptly when the Director of Public Prosecutions announced that the convictions of the 'seven' were 'unsafe and unsound', and the Home Secretary declared that they 'could not stand'. The Seven – six members of a family and one of their friends – had been given heavy sentences for their supposed connection with the Guildford and Woolwich public house bombings in 1974. Their conviction was based entirely on confessions extorted from two of the Guildford Four – released as wrongfully convicted in October 1989 – and the traces of nitroglycerin explosive said to have been found in swabs taken from their hands. Now the Director of Public Prosecutions conceded that 'The scientific evidence given to the jury may have misled them into excluding the possibility of innocent contamination, but . . . this was a real possiblity, however remote.' Such a grudging admission of error was widely felt to be inadequate in view of other facts that came to light, including the inexperience of the trainee who had analysed the swabs and the undisclosed fact that later tests had proved negative.

Meanwhile during June the IRA kept up an offensive in Ireland and abroad that cost the lives of several British soldiers and members of the Royal Ulster Constabulary. The offensive included bombings in West Germany and in Britain, where the Conservative Carlton Club was severly damaged. But in a series of dramatic incidents, police in Holland and Belgium succeeded in arresting three men and a woman suspected of IRA terrorist activities in West Germany; critics of the Irish Republic noted that earlier in the year the woman, Donna Maguire, had been acquitted and freed by a Dublin court.

OZONE CONFERENCE

AN international conference in London drew up new turn-of-the-century deadlines for phasing out the use of CFCs (chlorofluorocarbons) and other ozone-depleting chemicals. It also made the important decision to establish a fund to assist their phasing-out by Third World countries which might otherwise have been unable to afford more environment-friendly but expensive substitutes.

HUBBLE FAILS

LESS than two months after its launch, the Hubble telescope-in-orbit proved to be seriously defective. One of the lenses had been made to the wrong specification, giving distorted views, and it was revealed that – astonishingly – the two main lenses had never been tested together on the ground. Adjustments, if at all possible, would not be carried out for several years.

Another disappointing piece of space news was that, following the discovery of fuel leaks, all space shuttle craft had been grounded by NASA (the USA's National Aeronautics and Space Administration).

The Hubble telescope – an expensive failure?

BSE DEAL

A EURO-CRISIS developed in June when West Germany and Italy followed the example of France in banning imports of British beef and cattle. Their reason was given as fear of possible human infection by the brain disease BSE, although British spokesmen alleged that this was an excuse for sabotaging competition. Britain appealed to the EC Commission, which agreed that the bans were against the Community's laws; but they were only lifted when agreement was reached that all imports would carry certificates guaranteeing that beef came from BSE-free farms and calves from uninfected cows.

As the number of identified cases approached 15,000, a suspicious attitude towards beef persisted among the British public, despite government assurances that it was perfectly safe; many, but by no means all, experts agreed. The controversy was enlivened by the Minister of Agriculture, John Gummer, whose performances included a Bible-quoting, butcher-rousing, but poorly informed attack on vegetarianism and the well-publicized handing of a beefburger to his small daughter as an indication of his confidence in its harmlessness.

SDP QUITS

BRITAIN'S Social Democratic Party decided to dissolve itself after a turbulent nine-year career. Founded as a breakaway from an allegedly left-dominated and doctrinaire Labour Party, the SDP was led by four ex-Cabinet ministers, Roy Jenkins, David Owen, William Rodgers and Shirley Williams. For a time it seemed likely to rival or even overtake the Labour Party, and so achieve its stated ambition to 'break the [two-party] mould of British politics'. But its upsurge proved short-lived, and in 1988 the SDP majority voted to merge with the Liberal Party to form the Liberal Democrats. A minority, led by David Owen, fought on as an independent party, but in view of falling membership and financial difficulties, the disastrous 1990 local and by-election results convinced the leadership that it would be hopeless to go on.

Jaguar first and second at Le Mans.

SA EMERGENCY ENDS

IN South Africa, President de Klerk announced the ending of the state of emergency (and consequent restriction of civil rights) that had been in force since 1986. This met one of the main demands of the African National Congress, and so improved prospects for further negotiations. However, the state of emergency remained in force in Natal because of bitter fighting between black groups – a development that threatened the authority of the ANC, already somewhat affected by revelations about its brutal past treatment of dissidents and opponents. De Klerk's National Party also had its troubles, narrowly holding Umlagi in a by-election that made clear the growing strength of a Conservative Party bitterly hostile to the dismantling of apartheid.

AFRICAN TURMOIL

BY mid-1990 events in Eastern Europe and the USSR were influencing politics in many parts of Africa, where single-party rule had previously been the norm. In states as diverse as Gabon, Cameroon, Zaire, Ethiopia and Kenya, calls were heard for a multi-party system, or government statements anticipated such a development. This was so even in Zambia, where President Kenneth Kaunda was supposedly a revered father-figure ruling through his United National Independence Party. Months of student protests, given impetus by steep rises in the price of basic foodstuffs, culminated in an attempted military coup on 30 June. Kaunda blamed disturbances on advocates of a multi-party system, to which he remained bitterly hostile, but named 17 October as the date of a national referendum on the issue.

IN BRIEF . . .

- The House of Lords rejected a controversial War Crimes Bill that would have made it possible to prosecute German and other UK residents for crimes committed in Nazi-occupied Europe during the Second World War.

- 246 British football supporter who had come to Italy to see World Cup matches were deported for alleged misbehaviour.

- Checkpoint Charlie, a well-known crossing-point between East and West Berlin during the Cold War, was removed.

- West Germany guaranteed a large loan to the Soviet Union, and an EC summit resolved to study ways in which it could give economic assistance.

- In Algeria's first experience of multi-party voting, Islamic fundamentalists enjoyed major successes in local and provincial elections.

- The Jaguar team took first and second places in the Le Mans 24-hour motor race, repeating their 1988 victory.

- In Sri Lanka the cease-fire in operation since June 1989 was breached when fighting broke out between the Liberation Tigers – guerrillas from the Tamil minority – and government forces.

- Elections were boycotted by the opposition in Kuwait, where only a small minority of the population had the right to vote.

- The future of the Canadian federation was cast into doubt after the non-ratification of constitutional amendments recognizing the specific status of French-speaking Quebec.

- In Nicaragua the Contras – opponents of the Sandinista former ruling party – laid down their arms, ending the 11-year civil war.

- A peace agreement was signed in Spain between the Guatemalan government and opposition and guerrilla representatives.

Green light for

GREEN LIGHT FOR GERMANY UNITY

OBSTACLES in the way of German unification were cleared away with unexpected ease after a meeting between the West German and Soviet leaders. Economic and monetary union between West and East Germany had taken place smoothly on 1 July, giving the two states a common currency (the deutschmark) and bringing down customs barriers between them. But arrangements for political union seemed likely to be complicated by Soviet reluctance to see a united Germany join NATO, the 'enemy' alliance during the Cold War. However, after Federal Chancellor Kohl and President Gorbachev met on 16-17 July at Stavropol in the Caucasus (USSR), the Soviet leader effectively withdrew his objections. Given the momentum of events in Eastern Europe, Gorbachev was probably recognizing the inevitable, for as he told Soviet reporters, 'Whether we like it or not, the time will come when a united Germany will be in NATO if that is their choice. . . We were realists, we assessed the direction of change.' He may also have been influenced by the currently conciliatory attitude of NATO and the large West German loan to the USSR negotiated shortly before the Stavropol summit. Agreement was also reached on the phased withdrawal of Soviet troops from East Germany, and the two leaders looked forward to the conclusion of a wide-ranging German-Soviet treaty.

Once the crucial issue had been decided, rapid progress was made at the third round of the 'two-plus-four' talks. Arrangements were made for a German-Polish treaty guaranteeing the existing borders between the two countries, and for ending any vestiges of 'four-power' control over Germany. In a sense, this closed the final chapter of the Second World War, leaving the way open for all-German elections on 2 December and subsequent unification.

Soviet foreign minister Shevardnadze (l), Chancellor Kohl and (r) President Gorbachev take a break during their negotiations at Stavropol.

RUSHDIE FILM BANNED

THE affair of Salman Rushdie – the writer condemned to death by Ayatollah Khomeini for his allegedly anti-Islamic novel *The Satanic Verses* – took a bizarre turn when distribution of the film *International Guerrillas* was banned by the British Board of Film Classification. Ludicrous in content, the film portrayed Rushdie as a corrupt gangster, aided in murdering Muslims by Israeli thugs; he is finally struck down by divinely directed lightning. Rushdie declared his opposition to the ban, pointedly extending to his enemies a tolerance which they had refused him; and following his intervention the release of the film was allowed.

KENYA KILLINGS

THE suppression of a pro-democracy rally in the Kenyan capital, Nairobi, led to four days of rioting and many deaths. Subsequent repression highlighted the fact that Kenya remained a bastion of the one-party system at a time when political change was sweeping across most of Africa. In July alone, multi-party systems were promised in the Congo and Mozambique, and Chad held its first general election for almost 30 years. In Zambia the referendum on the one/multi-party issue was postponed, but there were signs of change in Zimbabwe, where a general amnesty was declared and the 25-year-long state of emergency was allowed to lapse.

German unity

LIBERIAN CIVIL WAR

IN mid-July Liberian rebel forces surged into the capital, Monrovia, and seemed set to topple President Samuel Doe. Led by Charles Taylor, the National Patriotic Front of Liberia had entered Liberia from neighbouring Côte d'Ivoire in December 1989, gathering support and advancing with unexpected speed in May and June of 1990. As living conditions deteriorated and atrocities multiplied, half a million Liberians fled abroad. Most of Doe's colleagues prudently went into exile, but the President himself rejected US offers to help him leave, and his troops dug in and successfully defended the executive mansion. Doe's presence was regarded as the main obstacle to a political settlement, although the situation was complicated by the existence of a rival group, led by Prince Yormie Johnson, which was hostile to both Doe and Taylor.

Rebel soldiers of the Patriotic Front of Liberia.

COUP FAILS

ON 27 July 120 members of a black Muslim group led by Yasin Abu Bakr attempted a coup at Port of Spain, capital of Trinidad and Tobago. They seized the prime minister, Arthur Robinson, and several other government ministers, occupied the Red House (the parliament building), and demanded the formation of a new government. Robinson and other hostages were wired up with explosives to discourage attempts to storm the building. There was a stand-off when security forces refused to concede any of the rebels' demands (even when the captive Prime Minister agreed to them), and on 31 July Robinson – who had been shot in the legs at the beginning of the coup attempt – was finally released. On the following day the rebels surrendered unconditionally.

RIDLEY SELF-DESTRUCTS

NICHOLAS RIDLEY, Britain's Secretary of State for Trade and Industry, resigned on 14 July following the publication of an interview with him in the *Spectator* magazine. According to this, he expressed his opposition to European integration with a startling lack of discretion, calling it 'a German racket designed to take over the whole of Europe'; if British sovereignty were given up to 'this lot', he declared, 'You might just as well give it to Adolf Hitler.' Such remarks about an EC partner and NATO ally made Ridley's resignation inevitable, and his cabinet post was taken over by Peter Lilley. Further embarrassment was caused by the 'leaked' record of a meeting at Chequers attended by Mrs Thatcher, Foreign Secretary Douglas Hurd and six academic advisers. In assessing the future role of a united Germany, the German national character was described in terms such as 'bullying', 'self-pitying' and possessing 'an inferiority complex', although these characteristics were mainly applied to the pre-Second World War period. Predictions of Anglo-German friction were falsified by the notable level-headedness of the German response.

GORBACHEV DOMINATES CONGRESS

STORMY debates were common during the 28th Congress of the Soviet Communist Party (CPSU), but the major splits predicted by some commentators failed to take place. With conservatives very strongly represented and radicals a vocal minority, President Gorbachev won backing for his key policies by personally chairing the most contentious debates and putting his case directly to the delegates. Gorbachev himself was re-elected as general secretary of the CPSU, and other party elections were regarded as generally satisfactory from his point of view. Leading radical Boris Yeltsin announced his resignation from the party, but his example was followed by only a minority even of delegates belonging to the radical Democratic Platform group. The long-term influence of these events on the Soviet Union's 19 million party members remained unpredictable; whereas Yeltsin claimed that the CPSU remained 'a party of bloodthirsty bureaucrats', Gorbachev roundly declared that 'Those who hoped that this congress would be the funeral of the Communist Party have been proved wrong.'

GERMAN WORLD CUP

THE main contenders for the World Cup displayed uneven form, and early interest centred on the Cameroon team, outsiders whose winning run took them to the quarter-finals. England won a hard match against them, then lost to West Germany in a penalty shoot-out after extra time had failed to bring a result. Argentina disposed of Italy but in the final two of their players were sent off and West Germany won by a single penalty goal, scored by Andreas Brehme in the 85th minute.

ALBANIANS LEAVE

FOLLOWING the suppression of anti-government demonstrations, almost 5000 Albanians took refuge in foreign embassies in Tirana, the Albanian capital. After negotiations the government agreed to issue the fugitives with passports, and they left the country.

The West German World Cup team celebrate their victory in the final.

CAP FITTED

IN Britain, controversy over the Poll Tax (Community Charge) continued as 20 local authorities were 'capped' – that is, were compelled by the government to fix a lower Poll Tax figure, in effect reducing their incomes and compelling them to cut their intended expenditure. The House of Lords (the highest judicial body in the UK) rejected the councils' appeals against the legality of the cappings. Soon afterwards Chris Patten, Minister for the Environment, announced extra government funding designed to hold down Poll Tax levels for 1991, which among other things was expected to be general election year.

NEW POLISH PARTIES

A NEW Polish political party, the Citizens' Movement for Democratic Action (ROAD), was formed to support Prime Minister Tadeusz Mazowiecki. This was essentially a reaction against the Centre Alliance formed in May to back Lech Walesa against Mazowiecki, and represented a new stage in the break-up of the artificial unity created by opposition to the previous Communist regime.

IRA KILLS MP

AS Northern Ireland Secretary Peter Brooke struggled to launch new 'round-table' talks on the future of the province, the IRA continued its offensive on the British mainland. On 20 January a bomb exploded at the London Stock Exchange; prior warning was given, the building was evacuated, and there were no casualties. Ten days later Ian Gow, MP for Eastbourne, was killed by a bomb which exploded underneath his car. A champion of the Unionist ascendancy in Northern Ireland, Gow was parliamentary private secretary to Mrs Thatcher before occupying ministerial posts until 1985, when he resigned from the government because the Anglo-Irish agreement involved the Irish Republic in the affairs of the North. According to the IRA Gow had played a central role in making British government policy during the early 1980s, and was still close to the Prime Minister – facts which they evidently thought sufficient to justify his murder.

TENNIS RECORD

AT Wimbledon the men's singles championship was won for the second time by Sweden's Stefan Edberg, but only after a cliff-hanging match in which defending champion Boris Becker came back from two sets down. Final result: 6–1, 6–2, 3–6, 3–6, 6–4. The outcome of the women's singles was even more notable, since number one seed Steffi Graf had been eliminated by Zina Garrison, who went down 6–4, 6–1 to Martina Navratilova, giving the Czech-born player a record ninth singles title.

Stefan Edberg, Wimbledon men's singles champion for the second time.

LEBANON FLARE-UP

LEBANON again sank into political and military disarray, with the breakdown of negotiations between President Hrawa and former Commander-in-Chief General Aoun, renewed fighting in southern Lebanon between rival Muslim militias, and Israeli air strikes against Palestinian bases.

NUM REPORT

ARTHUR SCARGILL, President of the National Union of Mineworkers, was severely criticized in a report commissioned by his union's executive following accusations made against him and General Secretary Peter Heathfield in March. The report concluded that Scargill had not used funds donated during the 1984-85 miners' strike for personal gain, but had nevertheless misapplied them; Scargill, however, claimed that his secretive practices and double accounting had been necessary to preserve union funds from sequestration during the strike. Allegations that he had received cash from Libya were unsubstantiated, but the NUM began efforts to secure about a million pounds, donated by Soviet miners, which it believed had been intended for the union, but which was held in bank accounts by the International Miners' Organization, whose president was Arthur Scargill.

IN BRIEF . . .

- In Britain, over two tonnes of CFCs leaked from an Oxfordshire research station.
- Golfer Nick Faldo followed up his victory in the US Masters by winning the British Open.
- Cricket: England won the Third Test, and with it the series, against New Zealand.
- The televising of proceedings in the British House of Commons was judged to have been a success, and was consequently to become permanent.
- Meeting in London, NATO heads of state offered 'the hand of friendship' to their former Eastern bloc adversaries, but insisted that the Organization's nuclear weapons would remain essential to maintain peace.
- Former dissident Vaclav Havel, interim president of Czechoslovakia, was re-elected for a two-year term.
- Iraq unexpectedly released Daphne Parish, the British nurse sentenced to 15 years in prison for assisting the alleged spy Farzad Bazoft, executed in March.
- In Saudi Arabia, the annual pilgrimmage (Haj) to Mecca was marred by disaster when a tunnel collapsed, killing over 1400 pilgrims.
- The first free, multi-party elections were held in Mongolia, resulting in a comfortable victory for the ruling (Communist) Mongolian People's Revolutionary Party.
- There were thousands of casualties as a result of an earthquake in the northern Philippines which severely damaged the cities of Cabanatuan and Baguio.
- Argentina and Brazil agreed to establish a common market by 1995; a similar agreement was reached for their own area by the Arab Maghreb Union countries (Algeria, Tunisia, Morocco, Libya, Mauretania).

Gulf crisis: Iraq

GULF CRISIS: IRAQ INVADES KUWAIT

ON 2 August the Iraqi army invaded and overran Iraq's neighbour, Kuwait. Most of the world's governments, including all the great powers, condemned this act of aggression, and the United Nations Security Council passed resolutions that led to the enforcement of economic sanctions against Iraq. With the rapid build-up of a multinational United Nations force in Saudi Arabia, it became clear that this was likely to be the most serious crisis of 1990.

BACKGROUND

A one-party state, Iraq was ruled by President Saddam Hussein, who had already proved himself a ruthless and ambitious leader. In 1988, at the end of a punishing eight-year war against Iran, Iraq's economy was very badly damaged; but her battle-hardened army remained the most powerful in the Arab world, and it was further strengthened by purchases abroad of technologically advanced weaponry.

This provided Saddam's most convincing 'argument' in the campaign he launched against Kuwait in July 1990. Both Iraq and Kuwait were major oil exporters, and as such belonged to OPEC (the Organization of Petroleum Exporting Countries). Iraq claimed, with a good deal of justification, that Kuwait and the United Arab Emirates (UAE) had produced far more than the quotas fixed by OPEC, and were consequently to blame for the slump in world prices. A meeting of OPEC at which the price per barrel was raised by $3 to $21 seemed a long step forward towards solving the problem, but the Iraqis went on to raise a new set of demands. They argued that wartime loans made by Kuwait to Iraq should be cancelled, since Kuwait had grown rich while Iraq had been fighting on behalf of the entire Arab nation against Iran – an interpretation of the Iraqi role that was open to dispute. Furthermore Kuwait was said to have stolen oil worth billions of dollars by encroaching on parts of the Rumeilah oilfield on the border

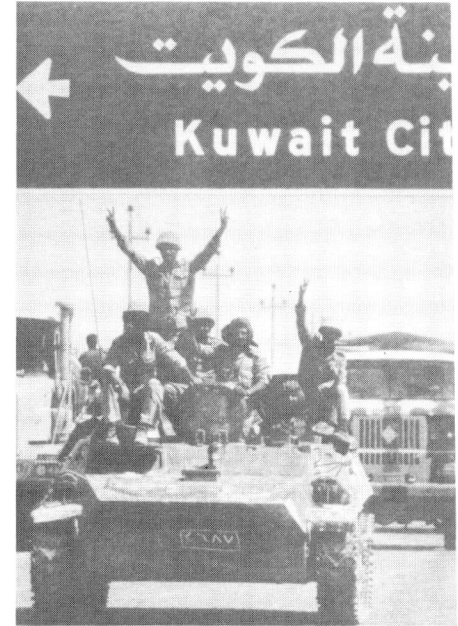

Iraqi forces enter Kuwait.

areas claimed by Iraq. The build-up of Iraq's forces on their borders evidently persuaded the Kuwaitis that they would have to buy off Saddam; but negotiations at Jeddah (Saudi Arabia) on 30 July were quickly broken off when it became clear that the two sides were impossibly far apart.

In view of the immediate invasion that followed, it is possible that the Iraqis never intended them to succeed. Both the Kuwaitis and most outside observers seem to have misread Saddam's intentions, imagining that he had blackmail rather than conquest in mind, especially in view of his recent threats against Israel and deteriorating relations with the West (for example, over nuclear triggers, the Bazoft hanging and the supergun affair). In the issue of the *Guardian* published on the morning of 2 August – by which time hostilities had actually begun – a correspondent gave it as his opinion that 'If the troops do move, the likelihood is that they will go no further than the oilfield of Rumeilah . . . straddling the existing frontier'.

Saddam Hussein, president of Iraq.

invades Kuwait

THE INVASION

AT 2 a.m. on 2 August, Iraqi troops and armour crossed the border with Kuwait and began advancing across the desert. About five hours later they penetrated the capital, Kuwait City, while Iraqi planes attacked military targets and the airport. Fighting lasted all day, but the Kuwaitis were able to put up significant resistance only around the city barracks and the Emir's palace while the royal family fled by helicopter to Saudi Arabia. Like most forms of news coming out of Kuwait from this time, casualty figures varied widely according to their source and were impossible to verify. Sporadic resistance continued for a time, apparently succeeded by some 'underground' activity, although again it was impossible to assess its scale and significance.

Attempting to justify the invasion, Iraq claimed that it was a temporary measure, undertaken at the request of Kuwaiti revolutionaries engaged in overthrowing the autocratic Emir. A Provisional Free Kuwait Government was formed – although some sources claimed that it was headed by Saddam's brother-in-law! – and an Iraqi withdrawal was first scheduled for 5 August and then said to have begun. However, this was either a ruse to gain time or a strategy defiantly abandoned in the face of international hostility and sanctions. On 7 August the new government declared Kuwait a republic and requested a union with Iraq, which duly took place on the following day. As most outsiders saw it, Iraq had simply annexed Kuwait.

The remains of an Iraqi helicopter shot down during the invasion of Kuwait.

WORLD REACTION

THE international community responded swiftly and with near-unanimity. The United Nations Security Council passed a series of resolutions culminating in the imposition of sactions on 6 August: all investment in Iraq and trade with her was to end, except for humanitarian supplies such as medicines. It was notable that all five permanent members of the Security Council (USA, USSR, UK, China, France), so often at odds in the past, were in agreement. Of the other members, only Yemen and Cuba abstained on some issues.

At a meeting of the Arab League, 14 of the 21 members also condemned Iraq. However, all Arab states were reluctant to see Western military intervention, and seven League members were either pro-Iraq or at least so anti-Western that they preferred not to associate themselves completely with the United Nations' stance. The seven were Jordan, the Palestine Liberation Organization (PLO), Yemen, Sudan, Libya, Tunisia and Algeria.

Alleging that Iraqi troops were massing on Kuwait's border with Saudi Arabia, the United States announced on 7 August that it would send ground and air forces to help the Saudis defend themselves in the event of an attack. The Iraqis denied any intention of invading Saudi Arabia, but this was not necessarily convincing in view of Saddam's past record (in July, for example, he had assured President Mubarak of Egypt that there was no question of Iraq taking military action against Kuwait). Britain also agreed to send troops to Saudi Arabia, and within weeks other countries had decided to contribute, creating a multinational military presence; the arrival of contingents from Egypt, Morocco and Syria was viewed as particularly significant in demonstrating that this was not an anti-Arab or 'imperialist' operation. By the end of August United States personnel in Saudi Arabia numbered some 40,000 in total, with more on the way, and foreign troops had also been accepted by the other unoccupied Arab states in the Gulf (Oman, UAE, Qatar, Bahrain). These operations were said to be purely defensive, and certainly any threat to Iraq (said to possess a million-strong army) was potential rather than immediate. The effective use of sanctions was strengthened by the US decision to begin a naval blockade that would prevent supplies reaching Iraq via sympathetic states such as Jordan and Yemen.

DIPLOMATIC MANOEUVRES

SINCE an Iraqi withdrawal would entail an immense loss of prestige and, almost certainly, his own downfall, Saddam Hussein was left with little room for manoeuvre. In an attempt to appeal to the Arab masses, on 12 August he proposed a general settlement involving a series of withdrawals, beginning with the withdrawal of Israel from her occupied territories and Syria's withdrawal from Lebanon. The longest-standing occupation should be dealt with first, so Kuwait would be the last on the list! (Nor did the 'arrangements' referred to in the case of Kuwait – unlike the other cases – include a clear promise that Iraq would actually pull out.)

Saddam's efforts to obscure the issue by linking his aggression with other problems found little response among governments. But demonstrations in a number of Arab countries showed that he had had considerable success in projecting himself as a champion of the Arabs against Israel, the 'reactionary' Arab states, and the West. Arabs asked why the West had done so little about the Palestinian problem over the decades, but had acted decisively when a despotic emir was overthrown. Understandably they believed that the answer lay in the West's vital interest in Gulf oil rather than its lofty principles. Support for Iraq was also fuelled by the despair of the PLO, whose recent moderation had produced no more solid results than its earlier militancy: as the upsetter of the status quo, Saddam seemed to be the Palestinians' only hope, and the PLO became his staunchest ally. Enthusiastic popular support for Iraq was also apparent in Jordan, where King Hussein tried desperately to be conciliatory to the United States without abandoning Iraq, his ally and economic partner. Jordan's position was made even more difficult by the huge number of refugees pouring into the country from Kuwait.

Saddam's other major move (14 August) was to accept Iran's terms for peace, withdrawing Iraqi troops from Iranian territory and accepting the division of the disputed Shatt al Arab waterway between the two countries. This represented a climb-down by Iraq, but it released 20 or more Iraqi divisions that might be needed in the new crisis moreover the waterway was less important to Iraq now that its control of Kuwait gave it an alternative route into the Gulf. For the moment, at least, peace did not lessen Iran's support for sanctions against Iraq, although Iranian hostility to a US presence made it hard to predict her future attitude.

HOSTAGE CRISIS

IN the West, the fate of foreigners trapped in Kuwait became a highly emotive issue. The borders of Iraq and Kuwait were closed on 9 August, and three days later a British man was shot dead attempting to escape. From 18 August Westerners in Kuwait were rounded up and taken to Iraq, and on the 20th it was announced that some of them were being held at various military bases; this made them not only hostages but a 'human shield', doomed in the event of strikes against the bases. Western indignation was fuelled by TV footage of Saddam Hussein with his 'guests', and was not much appeased by an announcement on 28 August that all foreign women

The grounds of the British embassy in Baghdad provide refuge for expatriates avoiding capture by Iraqi forces.

and children would be allowed to leave Iraq.

Another possible flashpoint was the beleaguered situation of foreign embassies in Kuwait. Iraq insisted they must be closed (since Kuwait no longer existed as an independent state), and when many refused to move to Baghdad they were surrounded by Iraqi troops. As yet, however, there was no attempt to storm them.

The immediate effects of the crisis were dramatic new alignments in the Middle East, including peace between Iraq and Iran, renewed PLO militancy and an alliance between the 'reactionary' monarchy of Saudi Arabia, 'moderate' Egypt and 'radical' Syria. Since Iraqi and Kuwaiti production was no longer

available on the world market, the price of oil soared to $30 a barrel. Plans to make good the shortfall were dependent on increased production by the (possibly threatened) Saudi fields, and the long-term consequences of the crisis for the world remained impossible to predict.

INDIA'S JOBS CRISIS

INDIA's Prime Minster, V.P. Singh, rode out the crisis caused by his dismissal of a controversial deputy prime minister, Devi

Lal. But much wider and more violent opposition erupted when he announced that 27 per cent of public sector jobs would in future be reserved for members of India's socially and educationally underprivileged castes. The intention was counteract the injustice of the caste system, which determined a person's status at birth. Although Singh's proposal had been recommended by a commission almost a decade earlier, governments during the 1980s had shelved it, fearing the political consequences. These became obvious as students and other high-caste groups rioted and attacked police, bringing into question the future of Singh and his coalition government.

US BUDGET CRISIS

AFTER months of acrimonious talks, the President and Congress failed to agree on a US budget that would reduce the country's huge deficit; it was estimated that, as matters stood, government expenditure in the year 1990-91 would outstrip income by some $168,000 million. Although President Bush had agreed to go back on his pre-election pledge not to raise taxes, Republicans and Democrats continued to manoeuvre, each trying to make the other seem responsible for bringing forward unpopular measures. Meanwhile the Gulf crisis raised the spectre of further, perhaps huge, expenditure.

GUINNESS CONVICTIONS

AT Southwark Crown Court, four prominent British businessmen were found guilty of false accounting, theft and conspiracy during the 1986 takeover of the Distillers' Company by Guinness, and were sentenced to varying terms of imprisonment and/or fined heavily. The offences were committed as part of an illegal share support operation – that is, an operation dishonestly to raise the price of shares above their true market value. In this case the object was to persuade Distillers' shareholders to trade in their holdings for Guinness shares. One defendant's £5 million fine was the heaviest ever imposed by a British court.

UK HEATWAVE

ON the third day of Britain's hottest-ever August, a weather station at Nailstone, Leicestershire, registered a record temperature of 37°C (99°F). Even fiercer temperatures in other countries (for example Italy and Greece) caused droughts and water rationing, fires, crop failures and deaths.

ONE GERMANY CLOSER

DESPITE political infighting ending in the withdrawal of the Social Democrats from the East German government, the move towards a unified Germany continued to accelerate. After intensive negotiations the date for unification was brought forward to 3 October. All-German elections remained scheduled for 2 December.

Former Guinness Chairman Ernest Saunders (centre) with his daughter Joanna and son James arrive at Southwark Crown Court during the Guinness fraud trial.

BHUTTO SACKED

AFTER less than two years in office, Pakistan's prime minister, Benazir Bhutto, was abruptly dismissed by President Ishaq Khan. The National Assembly was dissolved, a state of emergency declared, and the leader of the opposition, Mustapha Jatoi, appointed prime minister. Explaining his decision, the President accused the outgoing government of being riddled with corruption and utterly incompetent. There appeared to be a good deal of truth in this, especially in view of the Bhutto family presence in the government and the ostentatious life-style of many figures connected with Bhutto's Pakistan People's Party (PPP). Bhutto's election in December 1988 had ended eleven years of military rule and seemed to offer troubled Pakistan a new democratic beginning. But she subsequently failed to tackle the country's admittedly stupendous economic problems, mishandled the Sind disturbances in May, and at the same time alienated the Muslim clergy and the still-entrenched military, who were widely believed to be behind the sacking. Bhutto herself denounced the President's 'constitutional coup' and predicted that the PPP would win the election scheduled for 24 October.

SA TRUCE

IN view of positive developments in South Africa, the African National Congress (ANC) formally suspended the 'armed struggle' to which it had been committed for the previous 29 years. On the government side, arrangements continued to be made for the release of political prisoners and the return of exiles. However, violence in Soweto and other townships (mainly between supporters of the ANC and the Zulu Inkatha movement) had by this time cost over 500 lives, threatening prospects for further advances towards a multiracial society.

SOVIET DISUNION

ARMENIA became the latest in a steadily lengthening list of Soviet republics to proclaim itself a sovereign state within the USSR; in this instance, the wording of the declaration suggested that the republic's government contemplated quitting the Soviet Union altogether. Meanwhile it became clear that nationalism might be a force for disintegration at republic level too, as ethnic minorities within Moldavia and Georgia attempted to break away and form their own states.

HOSTAGES FREED

AFTER weeks of rumours and disappointed hopes, the Irish hostage Brian Keenan was released in Beirut, Lebanon, on 24 August; a teacher at the American University of Beirut, he had been kidnapped in April 1986, probably by the Islamic Jihad underground group. Hopes that other hostages might soon go free were raised by the helpful role played in the affair by Iran, and by the earlier release of two Swiss Red Cross workers who has been held since October 1989; a likely stumbling block was the Iranian demand that prisoners held by Israel should be released in return.

IN BRIEF . . .

- In Britain, the case of the 'Birmingham Six' was referred back to the Court of Appeal.
- BBC's new Radio 5 channel went on the air.
- 'Hackers', who use their computers to disrupt other people's systems, became liable to prosecution under Britain's Computer Misuse Act.
- A drawn Third Test at Lord's left England 1–0 series victors over India, which had, however, won the one-day Texaco trophy.
- In Yugoslavia, an explosion at the Kreka coal mine killed at least 170; only three men were brought out alive.
- Demonstrators in many Soviet cities protested against cigarette shortages, and the man held responsible, First Deputy Prime Minister Nikitin, was dismissed.
- The United Nations Security Council agreed on a plan to bring peace to Cambodia; it remained to be seen whether the warring Cambodians would accept it.
- The arrival of a West African peace-keeping force failed to end the three-way civil war in Liberia.
- Charged on thirteen counts, Marion Barry, Mayor of Washington, DC, was found guilty on one count of possessing cocaine.
- The US spacecraft *Magellan* was placed in orbit round Venus.
- The Honduras government used troops and tanks to end a six-week strike by banana workers.
- The 13-member Caribbean Community agreed to establish a common market from 1 January 1991.

US soldiers arrive in Saudi Arabia.

GULF STAND-OFF

BY September it was clear that there would be no early end to the Gulf crisis. The multinational force in Saudi Arabia was now formidable enough to deter an Iraqi attack (if that had ever been contemplated), but was nowhere near strong enough to evict the Iraqis from Kuwait. The US Air Force Chief of Staff was dismissed for publicly discussing an alternative military strategy – that of an air strike on downtown Baghdad to kill Saddam Hussein and his ministers.

The preferred option was to use sanctions to make Iraq withdraw. American and British determination to enforce the naval embargo was shown in a number of incidents involving the stopping and searching of Iraqi and other vessels. On 25 September the UN Security Council extended the embargo to air traffic, at the same time reminding member states that they must freeze all Iraqi assets (that is, not allow the use or withdrawal of Iraqi funds or property) in their territories.

Meanwhile the number of US personnel in Saudi Arabia rose steadily towards 200,000. Britain despatched

6000 men and 120 tanks of the 7th Armoured Division, known since their North African exploits in the Second World War as the Desert Rats. France, stung by an Iraqi takeover of the French embassy in Kuwait, sent substantial reinforcements, as did the Egyptians and Syrians. And Belgium, the Netherlands, Italy, Canada, Pakistan, India, Bangladesh and Argentina all sent troops or air or naval support.

The financial underpinning of the UN effort was even more impressive as an example of international co-operation, since it extended beyond the purely military aspect. The oil-rich Gulf states paid part of the cost of their protection. West Germany and Japan, which were not militarily involved, made substantial contributions, but they also – along with the European community, South Korea and Taiwan – provided funds to aid those Middle Eastern states that were suffering from the effects of the crisis: Egypt, Jordan and Turkey.

Apart from disruption of their trade with Iraq, such countries were injured by soaring oil prices and by the huge numbers of their nationals who could no longer work in Kuwait's oilfields. Money sent home by Egyptians, Jordanians, Palestinians, Pakistanis, Indians, Bangladeshis and Sri Lankans was a vital element in the economies of most of the states concerned. Moreover Jordan, and to a lesser extent Turkey, had a further burden in the hundreds of thousands of these workers who arrived from Iraq and Kuwait; Jordan in particular did not have the resources to feed and repatriate the ever-growing army of refugees that camped inside its borders.

Strenuous diplomatic efforts were made by US Secretary of State James Baker to preserve international solidarity; the delicate balancing involved became apparent when proposed US arms sales to new friend Saudi Arabia were scaled down after pressure from old friend Israel, which was at odds with most Arab states, whatever their alignment in the current conflict. On the other side, the Iraqis played the only cards in their hands, calling on occasion for an anti-Western

Stand-off

Fighter aircraft of the multinational force on a Saudi airfield.

Holy War (Jihad) and popular risings to overthrow the Egyptian and Saudi Arabian regimes, while at other times repeating that a settlement would be possible if it were linked with one dealing with the Israeli occupied territories.

Western indignation continued to be fuelled by the hostage and embassy issues. Although thousands of women and children were flown out of Iraq, several thousand Western men remained behind, of whom an unknown number were held as a 'human shield' at military installations.

At a one-day 'summit' at Helsinki on 9 September, Presidents Bush and Gorbachev agreed in demanding an unconditional Iraqi withdrawal from Kuwait. Although Gorbachev was visibly the more reluctant to contemplate a military solution, this united front, and references by both US and Soviet spokesmen to an emerging 'new world order', were very striking.

Presidents Gorbachev and Bush at a joint news conference after their meeting in Helsinki, where they agreed that Iraq should withdraw unconditionally from Kuwait.

CANADA'S INDIANS RESIST

IN Quebec, months of protests and obstruction by Canadian Indians were ended by police and army action. The trouble began in March, when Mohawk Indians at Oka put up barricades on a road to prevent the local council extending a golf course on to sacred land. Underlying the specific issue was discontent over land claims, poor conditions on the reservations, and Indians' lack of control over their own affairs. The

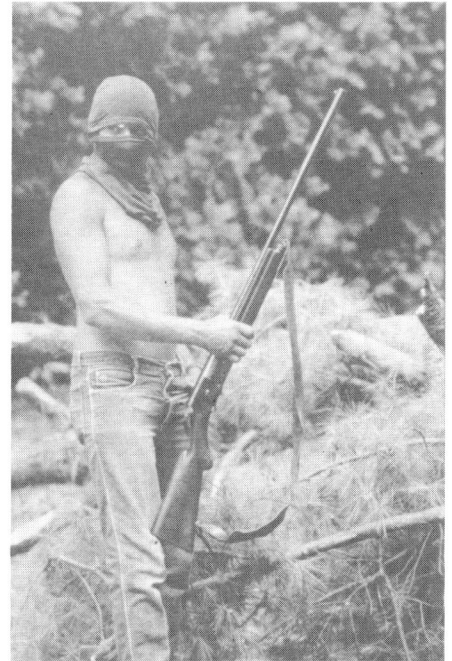

Armed Mohawk Indian during a land dispute with the Canadian government.

dispute escalated when other Mohawks barricaded a bridge over the St Lawrence River, causing severe traffic problems and angering the local white community. Concessions by the federal and provincial authorities failed to satisfy the Mohawks, despite reported splits between moderates and militants. But in September they capitulated to a show of overwhelming force. The barricades were removed, but confrontations and violence continued.

NEW PLAN, PLEASE

CONFRONTED with no less than three plans for economic reform, the Supreme Soviet (parliament) of the USSR failed to back any of them and asked for further proposals to be put forward. By contrast, the Russian Federation (the largest Soviet republic), led by Boris Yeltsin, opted decisively for the radical Shatalin plan, which visualized a speedy 500-day transition to a mainly private enterprise economy, and was to be implemented from 1 November. Whether the Soviet and Russian plans would be compatible remained unforseeable.

SERBS RAMPANT

NATIONALIST conflicts within Yugoslavia became even more acute as the militant Serbian Renewal Movement stepped up its activities. Demonstrations by Serb minorities in areas outside the present Serbian republic – already the largest of the Yugoslav republics – gave rise to fears that there might soon be aggressive moves to create a 'Greater Serbia'. A new Serbian constitution, in force from 28 September, was hardly reassuring, since it effectively abolished the autonomous status of Kosovo, where the Albanian majority had been restive all year. Kosovo's suppressed assembly attempted to declare the province a separate republic, but direct Serbian rule continued against a background of arrests, house-searches, strikes and boycotts.

WALLACE PAID

FORMER Northern Ireland information officer Colin Wallace was awarded £30,000 for wrongful dismissal after an inquiry conducted by David Calcutt found that Ministry of Defence officials had attempted to influence the Civil Service Appeals Board. The narrow scope of the inquiry was widely criticized, since it left unanswered most of Wallace's allegations about the smearing of MPs and other 'dirty tricks' or 'black propaganda' on the part of the authorities.

ANGLO-IRANIAN DETENTE

DESPITE unresolved differences between them, the United Kingdom and Iran agreed to resume full diplomatic relations, suspended in February 1989 after the Ayatollah Khomeini called for the death of the British writer Salman Rushdie. The new accord was facilitated by a declaration of British respect for Islam, made by Foreign Secretary Douglas Hurd, who was apparently satisfied by Iranian assurances that there would be no interference in British affairs as far as Rushdie was concerned, although the death sentence was not withdrawn and an alleged British spy, Roger Cooper, arrested in 1985, continued to be held in Iran.

DOE DIES

THE civil war in Liberia took a dramatic turn on 11 September when President Samuel Doe arranged to negotiate with rebel leader Prince Yormie Johnson. When delegations from the two factions met, tempers flared and in the shoot-out that followed 64 people were killed. Johnson's men evidently had the better of the argument. A wounded Doe was taken prisoner and later displayed dead and mutilated; reports suggested that he had been tortured and that his ears had been cut off. Doe's troops went on the rampage, chanting 'No Doe, no Liberia!' and inter-tribal reprisals added to the toll of massacres, rapes and burnings. With at least four post-Doe contenders for power emerging. The collapse of a fragile truce left a chaotic situation.

KAUNDA YIELDS

PRESIDENT Kenneth Kaunda of Zambia and his ruling United National Independence Party decided to introduce a multiparty system without holding the planned referendum on the issue. The enthusiastic turnout at meetings of the Movement for Multiparty Democracy evidently convinced them that it would be wise to yield sooner rather than later. It was planned to hold the first general election under the new system by October.

In neighbouring Zimbabwe, President Robert Mugabe continued to swim against the current by urging the formal adoption of a single-party system, but failed to convince his own ZANU central committee. However, ZANU's actual monopoly of power remained unchallenged.

SCARGILL CLAIMS VINDICATION

IN Paris a more or less amicable settlement was reached in the long-running dispute over the ownership of funds donated by Soviet coalminers during the British miners' strike of 1984-85. Alain Simon, General Secretary of the International Miners' Organization, produced documentary evidence to support his claim that the funds were intended for the IMO, and Britain's National Union of Mineworkers settled for a proffered IMO donation reported to be in the region of £742,000. The vindication of Arthur Scargill, president of both the IMO and the NUM, seemed complete when the Soviet miners' union took part in a unanimous vote of confidence passed at a meeting of the IMO executive.

TRAIN MASSACRE

AMID continuing township violence in South Africa, on 13 September unidentified attackers murdered 26 people and injured many more in apparently random attacks on the passengers of a commuter train on its way from Johannesburg to Soweto. A further shock came with the announcement that Winnie Mandela, wife of ANC deputy leader Nelson Mandela, was to be prosecuted in connection with the alleged kidnapping of youths belonging to a rival faction, one of whom died after a beating.

Bodies laid out on a platform after an attack on a train carrying black workers in South Africa.

BOAT PEOPLE DEAL

AN agreement signed in Hanoi appeared to offer a partial solution to the vexed problem of the 'boat people' – 53,000 Vietnamese who had fled from their native country to Hong Kong. Refused admittance to the colony, they were being detained in compounds, but the British authorities' efforts to return them to Vietnam had so far met with little success, since the Vietnamese were reluctant to take back those who came unwillingly; another significant factor was pressure from the United States, which strongly disapproved of such enforced repatriation. The new agreement envisaged the return of 'economic migrants' who had left Vietnam in search of a better life, but not of those who were refugees from political persecution by Vietnam's Communist government; these, by implication, could legitimately claim asylum. This distinction between political refugees and economic migrants (who were 'merely' in flight from poverty or even starvation) was being increasingly invoked as the wealthier nations became conscious of actual or threatened migrations on a large scale, for example from newly-free Eastern Europe to the West.

IN BRIEF . . .

■ At Milford in Staffordshire an IRA gunman seriously wounded Sir Peter Terry, who had been governor of Gibraltar in March 1988, when SAS security forces shot dead three IRA members.

■ Fire destroyed most of historic Eastgate, in the centre of Totnes, Devon.

■ English football clubs, banned since the Heysel stadium disaster (when 41 died after a wall and safety fence collapsed during rioting by Liverpool fans), played in Europe for the first time in five years.

■ The French Minister of Agriculture apologized to his British counterpart for attacks by French farmers on lorries bringing British meat into the country.

■ The final 'two-plus-four' treaty was signed in Moscow on 12 September, removing the last legal obstacles to German unification.

■ After an explosion at a nuclear fuel manufacturing plant, local authorities declared eastern Kazakhstan, USSR, an ecological disaster zone.

■ Despite the victory of the National League for Democracy (NLD) in the May elections, the military government of Myanma added to the number of imprisoned NLD leaders and showed no sign of relinquishing power.

■ Nepal's new democratic constitution came into force.

■ Torrential rains and floods in South Korea killed at least 130 people and left about 160,000 homeless.

■ A huge swing to the social-democratic National Democratic Party gave it control of the Canadian province of Ontario.

■ The United States announced troop withdrawals from Western Europe and the closing or scaling down of 151 European and Asian bases.

■ The city of Atlanta, USA, was chosen to host the 1996 Olympics.

■ New Zealand's Labour prime minister, Geoffrey Palmer, lost the support of his party and resigned; he was replaced as party leader and premier by Mike Moore.

Germany

GERMANY REUNITED

AT midnight on 2/3 October, Germany became a single, sovereign country for the first time since the end of the Second World War. The flag of the Federal (West German) Republic was raised outside the Reichstag, the historic parliament building in Berlin, and Chancellor Kohl declared that 'This is one of the happiest moments of my life.' The German Democratic Republic (GDR or East Germany) ceased to exist, and its armed forces were incorporated into the (Federal) Bundeswehr. East German premier Lothar de Maizière called it 'a farewell without tears'. But not all Germans rejoiced: some leading figures in the East, including former dissidents active in the overthrow of the Communist regime, complained that 'unification' amounted to no more than annexation by the Federal Republic, allowing the rapid run-down of the GDR's industries and the appearance there of mass unemployment. But although protesters staged a march in Berlin, the overwhelming majority of Germans were clearly in jubilant mood, taking part with enthusiasm in the nationwide celebrations.

The flag of West Germany flies over the former Reichstag (parliament) building in Berlin.

GULF: NO PROGRESS

THERE was little change in the gulf situation, despite protracted shuttle diplomacy by the Soviet envoy, Yevgeny Primakov, and the impact of the Temple Mount killings (opposite), which made the much-discussed 'linkage' of the Kuwaiti and Palestinian situations seem a more plausible possibility. Saddam Hussein released all his French hostages because of France's supposedly more flexible attitude to the crises, and British ex-prime minister Edward Heath visited Baghdad on a humanitarian mission and managed to bring out 33 ill or elderly hostages; but these Iraqi gestures had little or no visible effect on the attitudes of the US and its allies. The UN military buildup in Saudi Arabia continued, and in the course of the month President Bush's tone sounded increasingly impatient and warlike. Investigations by the human rights organization Amnesty International suggested that reports of Iraqi atrocities and torture in Kuwait were all too true; but Amnesty also found that some 800 Yemenis had been tortured in Saudi Arabia, whose anger at Yemen's pro-Iraq stance had also prompted the expulsion of hundreds of thousands of Yemeni immigrant workers.

AOUN DEFEATED

ONE of the factions keeping Beirut in a ruinous state of civil war was removed on 13 October when Syrian and Lebanese troops overran the eastern part of the city controlled by General Michel Aoun; the general himself took refuge in the French embassy at an early stage in the operations. Called in by Lebanon's President Hrawi, the Syrians were able to act with impunity, since their support for the US during the Gulf crisis made Western disapproval unlikely, whereas Aoun's Iraqi-backed regime was completely isolated. Hrawi's order to other militias to quit Beirut now seemed likely to be obeyed, opening up the prospect of a peaceful, undivided city for the first time since 1973.

Reunited

TEMPLE MOUNT DEATHS

THE Palestinian intifada erupted with renewed intensity after an incident in which Israeli police opened fire on a crowd of rioting Arabs, killing 17 people and injuring about a hundred. At the Temple Mount, a site sacred to both Jews and Muslims, some 3000 Arabs gathered to oppose an extreme Jewish group which planned to begin building a temple there. Police prevented the group from entering the area, but the crowd remained restive and violence broke out. Tear gas was used, Jewish worshippers at the nearby Wailing Wall were stoned, and the police fired – but there was disagreement about the sequence in which these events occurred, and consequently about who was to blame for the tragedy. The Israeli government claimed that the police had fired only when their lives were in danger, and hinted darkly that the whole thing was an Iraqi plot, while the PLO and Arab states denounced Zionist use of 'terror'. A United Nations resolution condemned the shootings, but a proposed UN mission to investigate how Palestinians could be safeguarded was refused entry by the Israeli authorities. Subsequently the country was again racked by riots, curfews, arrests, stabbings of Jews and

Aftermath of the Temple Mount killings in Jerusalem.

mob retaliation against Arabs. There were international repercussions too, since the Temple Mount shootings lent some weight to the argument that the UN should enforce all its Middle East resolutions, not just those against Iraq.

BHUTTO BEATEN

FOLLOWING on Benazir Bhutto's dismissal by the President in August, her Pakistan People's Party (PPP) was heavily defeated in national and provincial elections. The Islamic Democratic Alliance (IDA) emerged as the strongest party in the National Assembly and its leader, Mian Nawaz Sharif, became the new prime minister. Bhutto's charges of massive vote-rigging appeared to have been exaggerated, but the PPP was disadvantaged because of the corruption charges pending in the courts against Bhutto and her husband, the President's appeal to voters to support Islamic values (and, implicitly, to desert the secular, woman-led PPP), and electoral arrangements that gave Bhutto's party far fewer seats than the IDA although it had won roughly the same number of votes. The new prime minister was regarded as the favoured candidate of Pakistan's army, and it remained to be seen whether he would be able to take an independent line.

Benazir Bhutto campaigning in the Pakistan elections.

SINGH AT BAY

ALREADY in difficulties because of its stand on jobs for India's disadvantaged castes, V.P. Singh's government was beset by a new crisis as militant Hindus attempted to reclaim a disputed shrine at Ayodhya from the Muslims. The government suggested a compromise – building a Hindu temple beside the existing mosque – but it was rejected by the Hindus. And when Singh took steps to prevent a march on Ayodhya, the extreme Hindu Bharatiya Janata party withdrew its support for him, leaving his government facing almost certain defeat on a vote of no confidence scheduled for November.

EASTBOURNE SHOCK

A MAJOR political upset took place at the Eastbourne by-election, where a swing of 20 per cent caused the loss of this safe Conservative seat to the Liberal Democrats' candidate, David Bellotti. Eastbourne had previously been held by Ian Gow, the MP murdered in July by the IRA, and the Conservative by-election campaign implied that a non-Tory vote was equivalent to a vote for the IRA. Public resentment of this crass tactic was held to have caused the exceptionally large swing.

IRA'S HUMAN BOMBS

ON 24 October the IRA launched 'human bomb' attacks against British army targets in Northern Ireland. These involved forcing an individual to drive a van loaded with explosives to the chosen spot, where it could be blown up by remote control. The stratagem worked in two out of three attacks; the most serious explosion, in Londonderry, killed the driver and five soldiers.

ERM, NOT EMU?

AFTER months of rumours and disappointments, Britain finally entered the ERM – the exchange rate mechanism which fixed the value of European currencies within certain limits. This represented another step – rather reluctant on Mrs Thatcher's part – towards the economic and monetary union (EMU) which France and Germany in particular were anxious to achieve. Both the Prime Minister and John Major, the Chancellor of the Exchequer, claimed that joining the ERM was now feasible because the economy was responding to their policies and inflation was being mastered. As a further gesture of optimism, Major announced that Britain's very high interest rates would come down by 1 per cent.

Mrs Thatcher remained suspicious of the speed with which the EC countries were moving together, and hostile to ideas of a federal Europe. At an EC summit in late October she alone objected to plans for common political and defence policies. Equally objectionable were schemes for a single European currency, although Britain was prepared to envisage a common currency – 'the hard écu' – which could exist side by side with sterling. Alarming many of her supporters by taking up an inflexible position long before the issue became critical, Mrs Thatcher told Parliament that she would never propose the abolition of sterling, 'the most powerful expression of sovereignty a country can possibly have'.

BYATT'S BOOKER

BRITAIN'S most prestigious literary award, the Booker Prize, was won by Antonia Byatt's novel *Possession*. Shifting backwards and forwards in time, the narrative intertwines the lives of two modern literary researchers and the Victorian writers they are investigating, so that each of the two relationships illuminates the other.

EASTERN EUROPE'S TROUBLES

THE economic difficulties of post-Communist Eastern Europe were accentuated by oil shortages, caused by late Soviet supplies and steeply rising international prices triggered by events in the Gulf. Fuel was rationed in Czecho-slovakia and Bulgaria, while the Hungarian authorities more than doubled its price until striking drivers forced them to countermand the order. Ethnic conflicts continued to surface, most threateningly in Yugoslavia, where Slovenes clashed with the federal (central) government and Serbs in Croatia tried to establish their own self-governing region within the republic.

SOVIETS PLAN

ON 19 October the Supreme Soviet at last approved a plan to create a market economy in the USSR. The outline adopted was a compromise between the cautious Ryzhkov and radical Shatalin proposals, and it was not yet clear how (or whether) it would work in view of the Russian Federation's prior commitment to the Shatalin plan.

Meanwhile nationalism remained rampant in many parts of the Soviet Union, although in Azerbaijan the Popular Front, so powerful at the beginning of the year, was trounced in elections by the Communist Party. In Georgia, however, the pro-independence Round Table coalition won convincingly, and nationalist agitation in the Ukraine forced the resignation of the prime minister. The Moldavians, though anxious to secede from the Soviet Union, reacted ferociously to the declaration of a 'Gagauz Republic' by one of their own minorities, and Soviet troops were sent in to separate the two sides.

US BUDGETS

AT times the government of the USA seemed about to grind to a halt while the President and Congress haggled over a federal budget. With midterm elections due on 6 November, agreement was finally reached late in October. Intended to reduce a deficit that had grown to alarming proportions, it increased taxes on higher incomes and a range of consumer goods and services, cut health provision and other benefits, and made some economies in defence spending.

Ayrton Senna and Alain Prost crash, eliminating each other at the start of the Japanese Grand Prix. Since this meant that there was no chance of Prost overtaking Senna in the world championship table, the incident caused much adverse comment.

IN BRIEF . . .

- In the United Kingdom, police made a number of arrests on Merseyside in connection with alleged corrupt practices in local authority land deals.

- On 12 October the German Interior Minister, Wolfgang Schaüble, was severely injured when a would-be assassin shot him twice.

- Iraq and Iran resumed diplomatic relations, broken off in 1980.

- At least 120 people died when a hijacked Chinese Boeing 737 crashed into two parked planes when attempting to land at Canton airport.

- Somalia and Togo became the latest African countries to begin dismantling their single-party states.

- In New York, US Secretary of State James Baker and Soviet Foreign Minister Eduard Shevardnadze announced agreement on a treaty limiting their respective countries' conventional (non-nuclear) forces in Europe.

- Argentina prepared for a huge sell-off of state-owned industries.

NZ ELECTION

LABOUR'S change of leadership in September came too late to save the party from overwhelming defeat in the New Zealand general election. The victorious National Party was nominally more conservative than the outgoing government, but the specific policy differences were small, since Labour had used its period of office to introduce privatization, deregulation and other measures generally associated with 'right-wing' administrations; and despite economic problems and rising unemployment, the National Party proposed to continue along the same lines. National Party leader Jim Bolger replaced Labour's Mike Moore as prime minister.

Tories in

THATCHER QUITS: MAJOR IS NEW PREMIER

A political crisis within the ranks of Britain's Conservative Party brought about the fall of Prime Minister Margaret Thatcher, who had held office since 1979 and had led her party to victory in three consecutive general elections. This outcome was unexpected, despite the fact that Mrs Thatcher had been embattled for months. Her autocratic style of leadership, hardly challenged while the government was riding high, drew increasing criticism as Britain slid into recession, the Poll Tax provoked widespread discontent, and the Prime Minister maintained a hostility to closer ties with the EC that was not shared by most of her colleagues. The crisis was triggered by the resignation of her longest-serving cabinet colleague, and the crucial challenge to her authority took place at the Conservatives' annual leadership contest, which also effectively decided who was to be prime minister (because the leader of the majority party in the House of Commons always heads the government).

HOWE GOES

THE first shock was felt on 1 November, when Sir Geoffrey Howe resigned. A former Foreign Secretary and Chancellor of the Exchequer, he was now Deputy Prime Minister and Leader of the House of Commons – posts widely believed to represent a 'kick upstairs' (that is, a technical promotion that actually moved him away from the levers of power). Howe was also the last survivor of Mrs Thatcher's 1979 cabinet, and his resignation focused attention on the high casualty rate among her ministers, reinforcing the impression that she was impossibly difficult to work with. The point was driven home by former Defence Secretary

Michael Heseltine in an easy-to-decipher call for the cabinet to assert its 'collective wisdom'.

Hoping to dampen down the crisis, the Prime Minister and her supporters claimed that the resignation reflected differences of tone rather than real policy differences within the cabinet. But in his resignation speech on 13 November, Howe, usually perceived as a somewhat bland figure, savaged Mrs Thatcher for her habit of undermining government policies by casual or impulsive utterances of anti-European sentiments, and gave revealing glimpses of the struggles that took place within the cabinet. Appealing directly to former fellow-ministers sitting on the front benches, Howe declared that 'The time has come for others to consider their response to the very tragic conflict of loyalties [to the Prime Minister and to "the true interests of the nation"] with which I have myself wrestled for perhaps too long.'

HESELTINE STANDS

HOWE'S speech made a test of Mrs Thatcher's standing almost inevitable, especially since it came in the wake of a disastrous by-election result at Bradford North, where the Conservative share of the vote slumped from 39 to 16 per cent and the Tory candidate fell back into third place behind the Liberal Democrat. To make matters worse, the Chancellor of the Exchequer, John Major, for the first time admitted the existence of a 'modest recession'.

In the event there was only a single challenger to Mrs Thatcher in the leadership contest. This was Michael Heseltine, who had long been viewed (despite his denials) as 'waiting in the wings' to present himself as an alternative leader. Now he emerged with an alternative programme, putting at its

Geoffrey Howe, whose devastating speech led to the fall of Margaret Thatcher.

Turmoil

Michael Heseltine; his wife Anne stands beside him, announces that he will be a candidate in the Conservative leadership election.

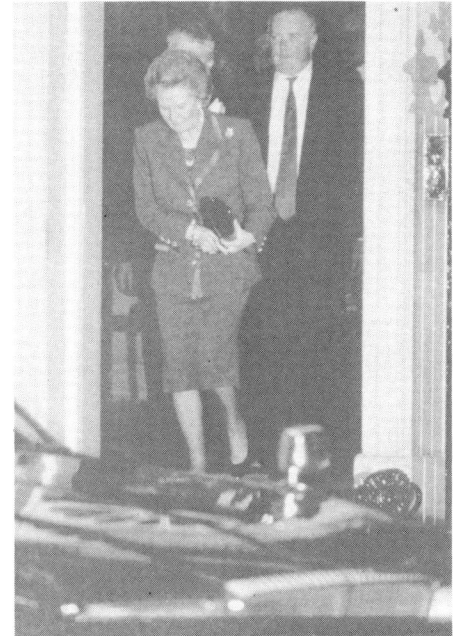

Mrs. Thatcher leaves 10 Downing Street after her resignation.

centre a 'fundamental review' of the poll tax, a thoroughgoing commitment to Europe, and selective intervention to boost the economy. Opinion polls indicating that the Conservatives could win an election under Heseltine, but not under Thatcher, helped the challenger's campaign, since the voters in the leadership contest were Conservative MPs, vitally concerned to improve their electoral prospects. On the other hand, support for Mrs Thatcher was very strong among Conservative activists in the constituencies, and MPs who openly backed Heseltine faced the possibility of being dropped by the local party (deselected) at the next election. Since the leadership vote was by secret ballot, however, MPs' actual intentions remained unpredictable. Despite impressive progress by the Heseltine camp, the general impression was that Mrs Thatcher would win, even though the contest took place while she was attending the European security conference in Paris.

EXIT THATCHER

MRS THATCHER did win – but not convincingly enough. At the end of the first round, held on 20 November, 204 votes had been cast for the Prime Minister and 152 for Michael Heseltine; 16 MPs had abstained. Unluckily for Mrs Thatcher, the rules laid down that a 15 per cent lead was necessary for outright victory in the first round. The Prime Minister's vote fell just four short of this target, and consequently a second round would have to be held a week later.

Returning to Britain, Mrs Thatcher told reporters 'I fight on. I fight to win.' But the size of the anti-Thatcher vote made it questionable whether she could ever present herself to the electorate as the leader of a united party, even if she won the second round. Either for this reason (almost certainly pressed home by senior party figures), or because her support among MPs was dwindling, the Prime Minister changed her mind and withdrew, effectively resigning as leader.

MAJOR WINS

THIS actually made Heseltine's task harder, for two leading cabinet ministers who had loyally supported Mrs Thatcher now felt free to enter the second round: Foreign Secretary Douglas Hurd and Chancellor of the Exchequer John Major, each of whom could hope to attract Mrs Thatcher's supporters and also some MPs who had voted for Heseltine as the only available challenger to her. It soon became apparent that John Major's campaign, begun more promptly than Hurd's, was gaining a rapid and unexpected momentum. When the second round was held on on 27 November, Major secured 185 votes, Heseltine 131 and Hurd 56. This time the front-runner needed only a simple majority, and although Major had fallen short of this by two votes, his rivals withdrew from the race and he was declared party leader. On the following day, 28 November, 47-year-old John Major was summoned to Buckingham Palace and became Prime Minister.

The new man – former Chancellor John Major.

Ireland's first woman president, Mary Robinson.

SINGH FALLS

THE beleagured Indian government of V.P.Singh collapsed as violence between Hindus and Muslim claimed hundreds of lives in many parts of India. The ruling Janata Dal (JD) party fragmented, a vote of no confidence prompted Singh's resignation on 7 November, and Chandra Shekhar, leading a 58-strong JD faction, became prime minister. The new government was entirely dependent on the support of Rahjiv Gandhi's much larger Congress Party, which had now recovered its traditional dominating position in Indian politics.

IRELAND'S WOMAN PRESIDENT

ONE of Europe's most conservative-minded Roman Catholic countries elected its first woman president – a left-wing lawyer notable for her involvement with civil rights issues including homosexuality and abortion. Mary Robinson benefited from the damage done to Brian Lenihan, candidate of the ruling Fianna Fail party, by a scandal in which he was held to have lied about making politically improper telephone calls. Dismissed from the cabinet when Fianna Fail's coalition partners threatened to desert them, Lenihan continued to campaign for the presidency but could not quite recover his lost ground. After her victory Mary Robinson congratulated the women of Ireland who 'instead of rocking the cradle, rocked the system'.

NEW UK CABINET

WITH opinion polls suggesting that his appointment as leader had caused a dramatic swing to the Conservatives, John Major formed his first cabinet as British Prime Minister. His post as Chancellor of the Exchequer was taken by his deputy at the Treasury, Norman Lamont, who had managed Major's leadership campaign. Douglas Hurd remained at the Foreign Office. David Waddington went to the Lords and was replaced as Home Secretary by Kenneth Baker. And Michael Heseltine, whose challenge had brought Mrs Thatcher down, became Environment Secretary; having been the first senior Conservative to criticize the Poll Tax, he was now responsible for reforming it. The absence of a single woman cabinet minister was widely commented on.

GULF: FORCE AUTHORIZED, TALKS OFFERED

AS the number of UN personnel in the Gulf approached 400,000, the coalition against Iraq remained firm; but there was a distinct change of mood. US opinion polls showed a falling away of support for a war, and the possibility of heavy casualties and disastrous ecological consequences was increasingly realized. While not changing his basic position, President Bush now stressed that 'we are giving sanctions time to work', effectively assuring the world that no immediate military strike was contemplated. And although both Bush and Mrs Thatcher had insisted that they were already entitled to use force, the US decided to seek a formal authorization from the United Nations for possible military action.

Meanwhile Edward Heath's visit to Iraq in October prompted others to follow his example. Like him, they were figures outside the political mainstream, and went despite the disapproval of their respective governments. The German ex-chancellor Willy Brandt, the left-wing British Labour MP Tony Benn and American ex-world heavyweight boxing champion (and Muslim) Muhammad Ali negotiated with varying degrees of success. Brandt, who subsequently opined that the US and UK should show 'a little bit more flexibility', secured the release of 189 German and other hostages; and when the German government also took a non-belligerent line, Saddam Hussein announced the release of all remaining German hostages. However, an Iraqi statement that all hostages would be released between Christmas and March 1991 was taken to be a time-gaining manoeuvre and received little attention.

After intensive diplomatic activity, on 29 November the US acquired the authorization it sought from the UN Security Council 'to use all necessary means' to make Iraq withdraw from Kuwait, if it had not done so by 15 January 1991. But the following day President Bush offered to hold direct talks with Iraq – something that he had previously always ruled out. In what the *Guardian* newspaper described as 'a speech notable for ambiguities', Bush insisted that no concessions would be offered, but that Secretary of State Baker would discuss 'all aspects of the Gulf crisis' – which might or might not mean some linkage of the Kuwaiti and Palestinian issues of a kind demanded by Iraq. On the other hand, the President declared that he was 'not hopeful' but wanted 'to go the extra mile for peace'.

BSP OVERTHROWN

STRIKES and student demonstrations brought down an accident-prone Bulgarian government. Like other East European countries, Bulgaria was in economic difficulties and desperately short of oil; the situation was made worse by Western hostility to the ruling Bulgarian Socialist (formerly Communist) Party, which meant that appeals for economic assistance met with little response. Since the BSP was the elected government of Bulgaria, its overthrow by street action and Western pressure did not bode well for democracy in Eastern Europe.

IN BRIEF . . .

■ The United Kingdom and Syria resumed diplomatic relations, severed since 1986.

■ Britain's National Union of Mineworkers rejected an overtime ban proposed by the leadership, 57 per cent voting against.

■ British Satellite Broadcasting, struggling since its launch in April, merged with Sky Television to form a new company, British Sky Television.

■ The 14-month-old *Sunday Correspondent* newspaper closed down.

■ All charges were dropped against the managing director of Walter Somers Ltd, one of the firms involved in the Iraqi supergun affair.

■ At the Conference on Security and Co-operation in Europe, leaders of 34 nations signed a Paris Charter envisaging 'a new era of democracy, peace and unity'.

■ Election results in the Yugoslav republic of Bosnia-Hercegovina followed strictly ethnic lines, with Communist and federal candidates losing everywhere to representatives of the Serb, Croatian and Muslim communities.

■ As the Soviet Union's economic and political difficulties reached crisis point, President Mikhail Gorbachev postponed his trip to Oslo to receive the Nobel Peace Prize.

■ In New York, extreme right-wing Israeli politician Meir Kahane, notorious for his racist views, was shot dead.

■ After weeks of violent disturbances in Bangladesh, opposition leaders were arrested and a state of emergency was declared.

■ The Democrats made modest gains in midterm US elections that were most notable for voter apathy: only 35 per cent bothered to turn out.

Gulf:

GULF: TALKS OFF?

HOPES for peace were raised early in December when Iraq accepted the US offer of talks; and on 6 December Saddam Hussein announced the imminent release of all foreign hostages, which was duly effected. This also ended the 'siege' of foreign embassies in Kuwait, which were closed on the grounds that, once the various nationals had been repatriated, diplomatic representation was no longer necessary. Plans for talks foundered because the US and Iraq could not agree on a date for Secretary of State James Baker's proposed visit to Baghdad. Iraq refused all the dates offered by the Americans, insisting on 12 January; but President Bush dismissed this as being too close to the 15 January withdrawal deadline, charging that the Iraqis were simply playing for time. Moreover Baker declared that any meeting would involve 'talks, not negotiations', his purpose being to make sure that the Iraqis 'got the message'; whereas Saddam Hussein continued to insist on a 'complete solution' of the Palestinian occupied territories question as a prerequisite and declared that there was no point in a meeting if Baker intended merely to repeat UN resolutions. Although it was revealed that US preparations would not be complete by 15 January, that date continued to be treated as critical. With Iraq known to possess lethal chemical weapons (already used against its rebellious Kurdish minority) and the US refusing to rule out the use of its nuclear arsenal, the outlook was fearsome. However, it was clear that many sections of public opinion – not least in the USA – were not convinced that war was justified or wise; and they were vocal and influential enough to suggest that at least one more serious effort would be made to achieve a diplomatic solution.

The Soviet crisis deepened with the resignation of President's Gorbachev's close ally, Foreign Minister Shevardnadze.

SOVIET CRISIS DEEPENS

FOOD shortages in the USSR became so serious that Germany, the EC and the United States all responded with aid or credits to help the country through the winter. The basic cause of these difficulties was not under-production but a breakdown of the distributive mechanism; this had apparently been undermined by economic reforms which abolished the old fixed-delivery system without replacing it with effective free-market arrangements. The situation was most acute in the big cities, although there was said to be no danger of actual starvation.

Against this background the Congress of People's Deputies debated the many problems of the Soviet Union and ultimately backed most of the proposals put forward by President Gorbachev. A new union treaty gave the USSR's various republics more say in central government, but separatist feeling remained so strong that six of the 15 republics refused to sign. The President was granted sweeping new powers to reassert central control, hold the union together, restore food supplies and crack down on corruption.

There was a new sensation when Gorbachev's closest collaborator, Foreign Minister Eduard Shevardnadze, announced his resignation. In a rather incoherent speech he complained about criticisms of his handling of foreign affairs, asserted that the tide had turned against Soviet reformers and predicted that a dictatorship was coming. His remarks appeared to be directed against certain figures in the army – people 'in colonels' epaulettes' – rather than against Gorbachev, whom he praised highly. Though guardedly expressed, Shevardnadze's fear seemed to be that Gorbachev would decide – perhaps under army pressure – to hold the union together by force, or would be replaced by someone who was more willing to do so. At any rate, Shevardnadze declared, 'I cannot reconcile myself to the events which are taking place in our country and the trials which await our people.'

Talks Off?

KOHL WINS

THE first nationwide German general election since 1933 was won by the Christian Democrats (CDU) led by Helmut Kohl. The CDU and its Bavarian allies received almost 43 per cent of the votes, while its coalition partners, the Free Democrats, advanced to 11 per cent. The result was a setback for the Social Democrats and smaller parties such as the Greens, but it was hardly unexpected, since Kohl's part in the drama of unification was evidently a tremendous electoral asset. It was widely recognized that this might change as the high cost of unification and its effects on East German society began to be felt.

Subsequently the Christian Democrats were embarrassed by accusations that Lothar de Maizière, CDU prime minister of East Germany, had dealings with the secret police of the former Communist regime. While denying the charges, de Maizière resigned his positions as Minister without Portfolio and deputy leader of the CDU.

Germany's first nationwide general election since 1933 was won by Helmut Kohl's CDU and its allies.

EAST EUROPEAN SCENE

THE collapse of the old order in Eastern Europe continued as riots and demonstrations in Albanian cities speeded up changes in a country that had once been ruled by the most isolated and authoritarian Communist regime in Europe. It was announced that political parties other than the ruling Party of Labour (Communist) would be allowed and an opposition Democratic Party was immediately founded. National elections were scheduled for 10 February 1991 despite protests that such an early date would not give the opposition enough time to organize properly.

Neighbouring Yugoslavia's federal structure seemed threatened with collapse as voters in a Slovenian referendum overwhelmingly supported secession. In Serbia, however, the Socialist (formerly Communist) Party won an unexpectedly convincing victory over the nationalist Serbian Renewal Movement; but since the Socialist leader Slobodan Milosevic, re-elected as president of Serbia, was also an ardent nationalist and federalist, conflicts with other republics remained.

The unity of Czechoslovakia was also threatened by Slovak militancy, but adequate compromises seemed to have been arranged by the end of the year.

Lech Walesa was elected president of Poland, but only after a disturbingly unpleasant campaign marked by anti-semitic outbreaks and abusive attacks by the candidates on each other's characters; in particular, Walesa's charges against his final opponent, Stanislaw Tyminski – that he was backed by closet Communists and secret police – smacked of witch-hunting.

In Bulgaria the political crisis was resolved for the time being by the election of a non-party judge as prime minister. But the governments of both Hungary and Romania looked increasingly embattled; and a deteriorating economy and constant street demonstrations prompted Romania's NSF government to open talks with the opposition about the possibility of forming a coalition.

TALKS AND TRADE: OUTLOOK UNCERTAIN

SERIOUS consequences were feared after the breakdown of the GATT (General Agreement on Tariffs and Trade) talks in Geneva, held in the hope of bringing down trade barriers. The conflict was caused by US insistence on a radical change in the European Community's agricultural policy; this was seen by Americans as unfair, since it involved subsidizing the Community's farmers so that they had an advantage in European markets over outside competitors, while being able to 'dump' (sell off cheaply) their surplus products in the US and other non-EC markets. Consequently the United States called for a 75 per cent reduction in subsidies over 10 years; but the EC offered no more than 30 per cent, calculated to include subsidies already cut since 1986. The situation led to speculation about a possible US-EC 'trade war'.

By contrast, the Rome summit of EC leaders was less fraught than expected. Making his first appearance as British prime minister, John Major was markedly friendlier and more conciliatory than Mrs Thatcher. Whether British policy on topics such as economic and monetary union had actually changed was another matter; it was not seriously put to the test on this occasion, since the discussions focused on aid for Eastern Europe and the USSR and the lifting of the ban on EC investment in South Africa.

CHUNNEL MEETING

WORKERS excavating from the French and British sides of the Channel Tunnel broke through and shook hands at 11.15 a.m. on 1 December, having created the first land link between Britain and the Continent for 12,000 years. However, the 'Chunnel' was not scheduled to be open to regular traffic until 1993.

Cheltenham Conservatives were split over the selection of black barrister John Taylor as their parliamentary candidate.

CHELTENHAM CLASH

INTENSE controversy arose over the adoption of barrister John Taylor as prospective Conservative parliamentary candidate for Cheltenham. Because Taylor was black, one local Conservative repeatedly railed against the selection of 'a bloody nigger', and as a result was expelled from the party. Discontent continued to be voiced on the more legitimate-seeming grounds that Taylor had been imposed by Conservative Central Office on the local party, which had never been allowed a choice of candidates.

RUSHDIE REPENTANT?

THE affair of Salman Rushdie, sentenced to death by Iran's Islamic authorities for his novel *The Satanic Verses*, took a new turn when the 43-year-old author was said to have become a Muslim. His conversion was effected by Harley Street dentist and religious activist Hesham el-Essawy, who began a campaign to win forgiveness for Rushdie. Despite promises that there would be no paperback edition of the book or further translations, Muslim reactions were unenthusiastic and the Iranian Ayatollah Khomenei declared that the sentence must remain in force.

UK'S RECESSION

THE year ended with forecasts of deepening recession in the United Kingdom. Inflation had begun to fall at last, but manufacturing output was declining, and unemployment rising faster than at any time since 1981. The balance of payments remained dauntingly unbalanced. High interest rates pinched consumers and also squeezed firms, with a record 24,000 going out of business; among the casualties were former crest-of-the-wave names such as the Sock Shop and Polly Peck.

Even the annual Christmas buying spree was more restrained than for some years past. One interesting result was that many big stores defied the law and risked fines by opening on Sundays in order to do as much business as possible; they could take comfort from Prime Minister John Major's stated belief that the Sunday Trading laws were in need of revision.

BURMESE CONFLICT

IN the face of continued repression by the military rulers of Myanma (Burma), the National League for Democracy, which had won the elections in May, set up a provisional government in rebel-held territory. The authorities retaliated by outlawing the NLD.

BEIRUT AT PEACE

BULLDOZERS destroyed the barricades in the Lebanese capital after the last Muslim and Christian militias dispersed or marched out of the strife-torn city. However, the new cabinet of national unity still faced an uphill task in uniting the various factions and persuading Syrian and Israeli forces to withdraw from Lebanese territory.

HAITI ELECTION

HAITIANS rejoiced as a radical Catholic priest, Father Jean Bertrand Aristide, won a landslide victory over more ortho-dox political opponents in the presidential election. Championing the cause of the poor in a country that had never properly recovered from decades of Duvalierist tyranny, Aristide was menaced by survivors from the former regime including the thuggish paramilitary Tontons Macoutes.

TAMBO BACK

THE 73-year-old ANC president Oliver Tambo returned to South Africa after 30 years in exile, receiving a hero's welcome. Although he urged a reconsideration of sanctions, an ANC congress voted to retain them; nevertheless there were signs that foreign investment in South Africa was reviving. Despite friction over these and other topics, both government and ANC leaders remained optimistic that fruitful talks between them would eventually take place.

IN BRIEF . . .

- In terms of share applications (some 12 million), the sale of Britain's electricity industry proved to be the most successful of the major privatizations.

- Severe blizzards struck Britain, stranding motorists in snowdrifts and causing loss of power and water supplies in thousands of households.

- In the case of the Birmingham Six, new evidence appeared to cast doubt on the original forensic findings and the validity of the confessions of the convicted men; but hearings in the Court of Appeal were held over to the New Year.

- Embattled Soviet President Gorbachev received his Nobel Peace Prize in the Kremlin.

- A Japanese passenger in a Soviet rocket became the first journalist in space.

- In India, hundreds died in continuing Hindu-Muslim violence.

- Mass protests led to the resignation of General Ershad, ruler of Bangladesh since 1982.

- Tamil Tigers declared an indefinite and unilateral ceasefire in Sri Lanka as 'a gesture of goodwill to promote peace'.

- Talks between the Cambodian government and the three resistance movements broke down over the role to be played by the United Nations in reorganizing the country.

- As rebel forces penetrated Somalia's capital, Mogadishu, the government of President Siad Barre appeared to be in desperate straits.

- Hissene Habré, President of Chad, fled as his army offered only token resistance to a sudden attack led by former commander-in-chief Idriss Deby, who took over as president and promised early elections.

- In Argentina, a military coup aiming to overthrow the government of Carlos Menem was suppressed.

Countdown to 1990: main events of 1989

JANUARY	George Bush become US president. Earthquake in Soviet Tadjikstan.
FEBRUARY	Ayatollah Khomeini, Iranian religious leader, passes death sentence on 'blasphemous' British author Salman Rushdie.
MARCH	Supertanker *Exxon Valdez* causes disastrous Alaskan oil-spill.
APRIL	Free trade union Solidarity legalized in Communist Poland. Big cities reject Communists in first free Soviet elections. Unrest in Soviet Georgia suppressed, but triggers year of ethnic violence in many parts of USSR. 94 die in crush at Sheffield's Hillsborough football ground. Poll Tax introduced in Scotland.
JUNE	Thousands of pro-democracy Chinese massacred in Tiananmen Square, Beijing. Overwhelming Solidarity victory in Polish elections.
AUGUST	Poland has first non-Communist government in Soviet bloc. West Midlands Serious Crimes Squad disbanded after malpractices revealed.
SEPTEMBER	Beginning of huge exodus of East Germans from Hungary, which opens borders with West; Poland and Czechoslovakia later follow suit. Communist Hungary schedules free elections.
OCTOBER	Mass demonstrations in East Germany force out veteran Communist leader Honecker, replaced by reformist Egon Krenz. 'Guildford Four', imprisoned as supposed IRA terrorists, freed. British Chancellor of the Exchequer Nigel Lawson resigns. San Francisco earthquake.
NOVEMBER	East Germany opens borders, making obsolete the notorious Berlin Wall (separating Communist East from non-Communist West Berlin); continued mass emigration increases pressure on regime. Entire Czech ruling body (Politburo) resigns. Long-time Bulgarian Communist leader Todor Zhivkov quits. Ruling Congress Party defeated in Indian elections; V.P. Singh replaces Rahjiv Gandhi as prime minister.
DECEMBER	Bloody revolution in Romania overthrows Ceausescu's Communist regime. United States invades Panama, overthrows dictator Noriega. Non-Communist government in Czechoslovakia. Bush-Gorbachev Malta summit hailed as end of Cold War. Repatriation of Vietnamese 'Boat People' from Hong Kong suspended after outcry.

People In The News

Baker, James (1930–)

US Secretary of State, in charge of foreign affairs, since 1989. Former lawyer, White House Chief of Staff and Secretary to the Treasury, 1985-88. Gave an impression of assured competence and dignity in building US–Soviet good relations and Gulf crisis diplomacy.

Bush, George (1924–)

US president (Republican) since 1989. Co-founder of Zapata Petroleum Corporation; US Vice-President, 1981-89. Has succeeded despite disadvantages (wealthy background, nervy manner, verbal clumsiness). Presidency notable for US–Soviet accord and US invasion of Panama.

Charles, Prince of Wales (1948–)

Heir to the British throne from 1952. Married Lady Diana Spencer, 1981. In recent years media interest has focused on his attempts to find a role other than king-to-be: speaking out on social and ecological issues, as critic of modern architecture (publishing *A Vision of Britain*, 1989), etc. However, in 1990 his badly broken arm (after a fall playing polo) made bigger news than his first one-man exhibition of watercolours at Salisbury.

De Klerk, Frederik Willem (1936–)

South African politician. A lawyer. Held ministerial office from 1978; Minister of Internal Affairs, 1982-85, and of National Education and Planning, 1984-89. In 1989 took over as State President, at first in temporary capacity, from ailing P.W. Botha, unexpectedly releasing Nelson Mandela and taking first steps towards multiracial society.

Gazza, (1967–)

(sometimes also known as Paul Gascoigne)

Footballer. Born at Gateshead, played for Newcastle, transferred to Tottenham Hotspur, selected for England squad. During the 1990 World Cup quarter-final, touched English hearts by bursting into tears after being booked. Result: media fame and fortune.

Gorbachev
(more accurately Gorbachyov)
Mikhail Sergeyevich (1931-)

Soviet politician. Rose through the Communist Party of Stavropol and Soviet Communist Party, becoming its General Secretary, and effectively leader of state, in 1985. Acquired other offices including new Executive Presidency, 1990. Introduced ambitious policy of reforms, including democratization of Soviet system, ended confrontation with United States, allowed dismantling of East European Communism and unification of Germany. But economic failures, nationalist movements in the USSR and rivalry of other radicals such as Yeltsin threatened his position. Has been variously assessed as sincere reformer and opportunist trying to preserve own power by manoeuvring between conservative and radical factions.

Heseltine, Michael (1933-)

British Conservative politician. In politics after a highly successful business career, became Minister for Environment, then Minister of Defence, 1983-1986, in Thatcher government. After disagreement with Thatcher and resignation, his leadership ambitions were an open secret; hence dramatic role in Thatcher's downfall.

Howe, Sir Geoffrey (1926–)

British politician whose ministerial career began in 1970. Closely associated with Mrs Thatcher as Chancellor of the Exchequer, 1979-83, and Foreign Minister, 1983-89. Appointment as deputy premier, 1989, widely seen as demotion; his resignation triggered leadership crisis and fall of Mrs Thatcher.

Kohl, Helmut (1930–)

German politician. rose to prominence in provincial politics, becoming Minister-President of the Rhineland Palatinate, 1969-76. Led the conservative Christian Democratic opposition to West Germany's Social Democratic government, 1976-82. West Germany chancellor (prime minister), 1982-90. Key figure in unification process, and first chancellor of united Germany.

Major, John (1943–)

British prime minister from November 1990. After career in banking, became MP, 1979, held minor ministerial office from 1983, then Chief Secretary to the Treasury (i.e. Number Two to Chancellor), 1987-89. As loyal and able follower of Mrs Thatcher, promoted to Foreign Minister in July 1989 reshuffle, then Chancellor of the Exchequer, October 1989, following Nigel Lawson's resignation. Won Conservative leadership in 1990 crisis as most likely to unite party; much was also made of (usually media-exaggerated) 'humble' background and grammar school education, believed likely to enhance appeal.

Mandela, Nelson (1918–)

Black South African leader. Son of the chief of the Temba tribe, Transkei. Educated at Witwatersrand University; became a lawyer. As ANC National Organizer, became convinced of need for armed struggle against all-white government and racist policies. In prison almost continuously, 1956-90. Following release, as deputy leader of ANC (effectively leader in absence of exiled Oliver Tambo), began dialogue with South African government of de Klerk.

Rushdie, Salman (1947-)

Indian-born British novelist, educated in Bombay and at Rugby public school. Won the Booker Prize, and recognition, with second novel, *Midnight's Children*, 1981, in 'magic realist' vein (mixing realism with fantasy). *Shame*, 1983, followed, but *The Satanic Verses*, 1988, provoked death-threats from offended Muslims, and thereafter Rushdie lived in hiding, protected by security personnel and under acute psychological pressure. Late in 1990 he converted to Islam, but it was not clear whether this would conciliate Muslims and allow him to live a normal life.

Saddam Hussein (1937–)

Iraqi dictator. Joined Baath Socialist Party and became veteran conspirator; experienced exile and imprisonment; twice sentenced to death. After taking a prominent role in the 1968 coup, rose steadily in the party and the governing Revolutionary Command Council. President of Iraq since 1979. Brutal suppression of rebellious Kurdish minority included use of chemical weapons. Led Iraq into indecisive, costly war with Iran, 1980-88. Partly an attempt to recoup, his invasion of oil-rich Kuwait launched 1990-91 Gulf crisis.

Shevardnadze,
Eduard Amvrosyevich (1928-)

Soviet politician. A Georgian, he rose through that republic's party apparatus. As Foreign Minister from 1985, closely associated with Gorbachev; prominent in US–Soviet accord and disarmament talks. His sensational resignation in December 1990 seemed possible prelude to serious political developments in USSR.

Thatcher, Margaret (1925–)

British prime minister, 1979-90. Research chemist and barrister before becoming MP in 1959. Secretary of State for Education, 1970-74; replaced Edward Heath as leader of Conservatives in opposition, 1975. Strong-willed, abrasive leader; after recession, recovered popularity through Falklands war victory, 1982; won elections in 1983 and 1987, weakening trade unions and presiding over wide-ranging privatization programme. In 1990 another recession and the new Poll Tax led to loss of popularity, and autocratic style and attitude to EC led to downfall. Widely different verdicts have been delivered on her personality and the policies of her government.

Walesa, Lech (1943–)
(pronounced Valensa)

Polish labour leader and politician. An electrician at the Lenin shipyard, Gdańsk, from 1966. As prominent labour activist, became co-founder and leader of Solidarity, the independent (non-government controlled) union that first challenged (1980-82) and ultimately played central role in destroying Poland's Communist regime, 1989. A fervent Catholic and anti-Communist with an aggressive personality, he became a controversial figure in post-Communist Poland, variously accused of egomania, anti-semitism and witch-hunting, but was elected president, 1990.

Yeltsin, Boris Nikolayevich
(1931–)

Soviet politician. A construction worker until 1968, when he began his rise through the Sverdlovsk Communist Party. Favoured by Gorbachev until he publicly criticized slow pace of reforms; consequently sacked from government post and leadership of Moscow Party. Elected against Gorbachev's opposition to Supreme Soviet, 1989, emerged as foremost radical. Presidency of the Russian Federation, 1990, gave him formidable position.

Exits

Among those who died in 1990 were:

Leonard Bernstein, *US composer and conductor*

Aaron Copland, *US composer*

Roald Dahl, *British writer*

Sammy Davis Jr, *US entertainer*

Lawrence Durrell, *British writer*

Friedrich Dürrenmatt, *Swiss playwright*

Greta Garbo, *Swedish film actress*

Ava Gardner, *US film actress*

Rex Harrison, *British actor*

Jim Henson, *US muppeteer*

(Sir) Tom Hopkinson, *pioneer photojournalist*

(Sir) Len (Leonard) Hutton, *England cricketer*

Margaret Lockwood, *British film actress*

Alberto Moravia, *Italian novelist*

Malcolm Muggeridge, *journalist, TV personality*

Luigi Nono, *Italian composer*

Tunku Abdul Rahman, *Malaysian leader*

Pat Reid, *British Colditz escaper*

A.J.P. Taylor, *British historian*

Paul Tortelier, *French cellist*

Eva Turner, *British opera singer*

Max Wall, *British actor*

Irving Wallace, *US writer*

Patrick White, *Australian writer*

Glossary

AMENDMENT	An alteration or improvement, used especially of changes to laws and constitutions. An amendment to an established constitution usually requires more than a simple majority before it is enacted.
AMNESTY	General pardon, often issued in states where reconciliation is being attempted after a period of widespread political violence.
ANC	African National Congress, the most important South African organization opposing the white supremacist policies of successive governments.
ANNEXATION	The formal act in which a state takes possession of a previously independent country.
ANTI-SEMITISM	Hatred of the Jews, or policies directed against them; opposition to ZIONISM is not necessarily motivated by anti-semitism.
ARBITRATION	The making of decisions on contentious issues by an outside, intendedly unbiased body; for example, arbitration is sometimes used to avoid a strike when employers and workers cannot agree on a wage claim.
AUSTERITY PROGRAMME	Political programme which involves the acceptance of hardships, viewed as inevitable or as the prelude to better times.
BLOCKADE	Seal off a country from outside by preventing supplies etc. leaving or reaching it.
BOYCOTT	To cut off all contact (most frequently economic) with a state or organization.
BSE	Bovine spongiform encephalopathy, or 'mad cow disease'.
CABINET	Relatively small group, comprising the most important ministers in a government, charged with making major decisions.
CFCs	Chlorofluorocarbons, chemicals that damage the earth's ozone layer.
COALITION	Group of political parties or states, banded together for a common purpose.
COLD WAR	The situation in which the West (NATO) and the Communist East (WARSAW PACT) formed intensely hostile blocs, prepared for a possible war with each other. With occasional thaws, the Cold War lasted from about 1947 to the late 1980s.
COUP	Attempt to overthrow a government – violent but (unlike a revolt or revolution) brief, by a 'blow' (French, *coup*).
DEREGULATION	The abolition of rules formerly imposed to control the conduct of a commercial or industrial sector.
DISSIDENT	A person who works and/or speaks out against the government, without resorting to violence, in countries where such actions are strongly discouraged or forbidden.
DRUG CARTELS	Organizations controlling the production and illicit movement of drugs such as cocaine; powerful enough in Colombia to threaten the stability of the state.
EAST GERMANY	See GDR.
EC	European Community, consisting in 1990 of 12 member states with an increasingly large range of common economic, legal and political policies; the former 'Common Market'.
EMBARGO	Prohibition of trade as part of a dispute or hostilities with another state.
ERM	Exchange Rate Mechanism; mechanism for regulating – and consequently stabilizing – the value of EC currencies against one another.
EUROPEAN COMMUNITY	See EC.
EXTRADITE	Hand over an alleged offender to a foreign government. Extradition agreements between states often lay down arrangements for the handing over of alleged criminals, but not for political refugees – but the distinction is often hard to make.
FACTIONS	Political groups; often used disapprovingly of groups within a party or movement whose activities are felt to undermine its unity.
FEDERATION	Group of associated states which retain their own governments while setting up a central (federal) government to run their joint affairs. The USA and USSR are federations; the EC may in time become one.
FUNDAMENTALISTS	Currently describes both Muslims and Christians who reject all efforts to reinterpret traditional doctrines and practices in the light of changing circumstances and values. Islamic fundamentalism has become a powerful political force since the fall of the Shah of Iran in 1979.
GATT	General Agreement on Tariffs and Trade; despite its name, not an agreement but a United Nations agency set up in 1948 to work for greater freedom of trade.
GAZA STRIP	See OCCUPIED TERRITORIES.
GDR	The German Democratic Republic, or East Germany; former Communist state which in 1990 became part of a united Germany.
GUERRILLAS	Fighters, usually confronted by a stronger enemy, who wage irregular warfare, using hit-and-run tactics etc.
INFLATION	Describes a general rise in prices; regarded as acceptable within limits, but if unchecked it has undesirable economic effects.
INTEREST RATE	The rate at which borrowed money must be paid for; high interest rates discourage consumer spending but also create difficulties for businesses and house-buyers.
INTIFADA	Unarmed and (relatively) non-violent 'uprising' by Palestinians in the OCCUPIED TERRITORIES, begun in late 1987.
IRA	Irish Republican Army; underground organization dedicated to 'liberating' Northern Ireland from the United Kingdom and making it part of the Irish Republic.
JIHAD	Holy War, to be waged by Muslims against non-believers.
LEFT-WING	Describes a spectrum of views, generally Socialist or Communist.
LIKUD	Right-wing party, the main element in Israeli governments since 1977.
MANDATE	Authority to act: a government is said to have a mandate to carry out policies which it advocated before being elected, but not necessarily for major decisions about other issues.

Glossary

MARKET ECONOMY	Economy in which the production and distribution of goods and services is determined by the supply-demand-price mechanism, as opposed to a command ecomony in which government decisions fix quotas, prices etc.
MARTIAL LAW	Military law, imposed on areas or countries in critical situations; it effectively reduces citizens' civil and legal rights.
MONOPOLY	Sole ownership or control.
NASA	National Aeronautics and Space Administration; the organization in charge of the United States' space programme.
NATO	North Atlantic Treaty Organization, the principal Western COLD WAR alliance, directed against the USSR and the WARSAW PACT.
OCCUPIED TERRITORIES	The West Bank of the Jordan and the Gaza Strip, occupied by Israel since the Six-Day War of 1967. With an overwhelming majority of non-Jewish Arabs, the Occupied Territories – especially the West Bank – are seen as the nucleus of a future Palestinian state, although Jewish settlement has raised the spectre of permanent occupation and annexation.
OPEC	The Organization of Petroleum Exporting Countries.
PALESTINE LIBERATION ORGANIZATION	See PLO.
PARAMILITARY	Describe non-military organizations that are run on military lines, often arming and carrying out acts of violence.
PERESTROIKA	Policy of 'reconstruction' of Soviet society, intended to make it freer and more economically efficient.
PLEBISCITE	A vote in which all electors take part to decide a specific issue.
PLO	Palestine Liberation Organization, the principal organization representing the Palestinians in their struggle for statehood.
PRIVATIZATION	The sale of public property to private buyers.
RADICAL	Favouring fundamental change rather than limited adjustments or improvements.
REACTIONARY	One who favours returning to a past political order; in practice the word is used to describe a person of extreme right-wing views.
RECESSION	Period of economic difficulties in which production declines and unemployment rises. If sufficiently prolonged and severe, it becomes known as a depression.
REFERENDUM	Same as a PLEBISCITE.
REPATRIATE	Send back to country of origin.
RIGHT-WING	Describes a spectrum of views from fascist to conservative; usually contrasted with liberal, Socialist or Communist views.
SANCTIONS	Economic boycott imposed to punish a country and persuade it to change its policies. Cutting off trade and investment in order to damage its economy is put forward as an acceptable alternative to war, but the effectiveness of sanctions has often been disputed.
SEPARATIST	Aiming to break away; usually describes a province, state or ethnic group wishing to leave (SECEDE from) the country of which it is part.
SEQUESTRATION	Setting aside or confiscation, not necessarily permanent. During the 1984 British miners' strike union funds were sequestrated when the National Union of Mineworkers defied the courts.
SHUTTLE DIPLOMACY	Diplomacy involving rapid and frequent travel by a leading government figure in order to negotiate at the highest level and defuse a crisis.
SOLIDARITY	Free trade union movement whose activities discredited and ultimately brought down Poland's Communist regime (1989).
STRATEGIC NUCLEAR ARMS	Long distance nuclear weapons intended for use against an enemy's cities and industrial and command centres.
TERRORIST	Term of disapproval, used of those who plant bombs or commit other terror-making acts of violence for political reasons, especially where civilian casualties are possible. 'Terrorists' regard themselves as 'freedom-fighters'.
UN	United Nations Organization (UNO).
UNILATERAL	Said or done by one side only; a unilateral ceasefire, e.g., implies that one side will cease hostilities without waiting for its enemies to agree.
US	United States of America (USA).
USSR	Union of Soviet Socialist Republics; the Soviet Union.
VETO	Prohibition with unarguable authority; any permanent member of the United Nations Security Council can veto a proposal, however well supported, making the Council powerless to act on it.
WARSAW PACT	Communist military alliance, equivalent to NATO.
WEST BANK	see OCCUPIED TERRITORIES.
ZIONISM	Originally described the movement to create a Jewish national home in Palestine. Since the creation of the state of Israel, 'Zionist' tends to be used as a term of abuse, for alleged Israeli racism and expansionism.

In & Out

In	Out
Major	Thatcher
British Sky	BSB
Yeltsin	Shevardnadze
Robinson	Lenihan
The European	*The Sunday Correspondent*
Guinness Three	Nelson Mandela
Chamorro	Ortega
Romantic movies	Blockbuster movies
Aristide	Avril
Poll Tax (England and Wales)	Nicholas Ridley
Cliff Richard	Jason Donovan
Hendry	Davis
New £5 note	SDP
Teenage Mutant Ninja Turtles	Sir Geoffrey Howe
Walesa	Jaruselski
Alesi	Mansell
National Power	Nationalized Electricity
de Maizière	de Maizière
Nawaz Sharif	Benazir Bhutto
Steve Backley	Sebastian Coe
Cameroon	Bobby Robson
Betty Boo	New Kids on the Block
Hip House	Acid House
Iliescu	Modrow
Carey	Runcie
The Australians	Larkins, Lamb, Smith, Gower, Stewart, etc.